THE MIDDLE AGES

MIKE CORBISHLEY

THIRD EDITION

CHELSEA HOUSE PUBLISHERS

An imprint of Infobase Publishing

Cultural Atlas for Young People
THE MIDDLE AGES
Third Edition

Copyright © 2007 The Brown Reference Group plc

Chelsea House
An imprint of Infobase Publishing
132 West 31st Street
New York, NY 10001

Library of Congress Cataloging-in-Publication Data available upon request.

ISBN: 0-8160-6825-9

ISBN 13 digit: 978-0-8160-6825-8

Set ISBN: 978-0-8160-7218-7

Chelsea House books are available at special discounts when purchased in bulk quantities for businesses, associations, institutions, or sales promotions. Please call our Special Sales Department in New York at (212) 967-8800 or (800) 322-8755.

You can find Chelsea House on the World Wide Web at:
http://www.chelseahouse.com

The Brown Reference Group
(incorporating Andromeda Oxford Limited)
8 Chapel Place, Rivington Street
London EC2A 3DQ
www.brownreference.com

For The Brown Reference Group plc:
Editorial Director: Lindsey Lowe
Project Editor: Graham Bateman
Editor: Virginia Carter
Design: Steve McCurdy
Senior Managing Editor: Tim Cooke

Printed in Singapore

10 9 8 7 6 5 4 3 2 1

Artwork and Picture Credits
All maps drawn by Lovell Johns, Oxford. Artwork by Adam Hook.

Key: t = top, b = bottom, c = center, l = left, r = right

Title page Alan Hutchison Library. 5 Dominique Martinez. 6–7 Malcolm Smythe. 10–11 Bridgeman Art Library. 14l Richard and Adam Hook. 14r BM. 16 Equinox. 17 Scala, Florence. 18 KM. 18 BM. 19 Scala, Florence. 20t Service de Documentation, Paris. 20bl Equinox Picture Archive, Oxford. 20br Leonard von Matt, Buochs. 21 Pierpont Morgan Library, NY. 22t Michael Holford. 22cl Norfolk Museums Service. 22–23 KM. 24 University Museum of National Antiquities, Oslo. 25 Richard and Adam Hook. 27l Bodleian Library, Oxford. 27r British Library, London. 28 English Heritage. 30 KM. 30–31 Michael Holford, Loughton. 32 Richard and Adam Hook. 33t Bodleian Library, Oxford. 33b National Monument Record. 34t A.F. Kersting, London. 34b KM. 36t Universitäts – Bibliothek, Jena. 36b KM. 38bl Sonia Halliday, Weston Turville. 38br Master and Fellows of Trinity College, Cambridge. 38–39 KM. 39t CF. 39bl CF. 39br Mike Corbishley. 40t Michel Vuillemin, Troyes. 40b Robert Harding Picture Library Ltd. 41 Bodleian Library, Oxford. 42bl Dick Barnard, Milverton. 42br KM. 42–43 Dick Barnard, Milverton. 44, 45 Sonia Halliday, Weston Turville. 46t Historik Museum, Bergen. 46b Michael Dixon, Dover. 47t Master and Fellows of Magdalene College, Cambridge. 47bl Kunsthistorisches Museum, Vienna. 47br Christopher Page, Oxford. 48t Ronald Sheridan. 48b History of Science Museum, Oxford. 49tl Österreichische Nationalbibliothek, Vienna. 49tr British Library, London. 49bl Mary Evans Picture Library, London. 49br Bibliothèque Nationale, Paris. 50–51 Bridgeman Art Library. 52t Michael Holford, Loughton. 52b Victoria and Albert Museum, London. 52–53 Bibliothèque Nationale, Paris. 53t Graham Speake, Oxford. 54t Bodleian Library, Oxford. 54b, 58 Bibliothèque Nationale, Paris. 58–59 KM. 60 Biblioteca Apostolica Vaticana. 62t Robert Harding Associates, London. 62bl, 62br Michael Dixon, Dover. 63cr Leonard von Matt, Buochs. 63bl Michael Holford, Loughton. 65l Franco Ragazzi, Bologna. 65r British Library, London. 66t Edwin Smith, Saffron Walden. 66b Robert Harding Picture Library, London. 68t Alan Hutchison Library, London. 68c Dick Barnard, Milverton. 68b Zefa, London. 69 CF. 70t Biblioteca Apostolica Vaticana. 70bl, br Bibliothèque Nationale, Paris. 71 Musée Condé, Chantilly. 72 Michael Holford, Loughton. 73 Sonia Halliday, Weston Turville. 74l University Library, Ghent. 74r Public Record Office, London. 75 KM. 76tr Andrew Lawson, Oxford. 76cr Leonard von Matt, Buochs. 76bl Graham Speake, Oxford. 77 John Fuller, Cambridge. 78t Zefa, London. 78c Dorian Gerhold, London. 78b Dr L. Beckel, Bad Ischl, Austria. 80 Fairford, Glos. 80–81 KM. 81t,b Sonia Halliday, Weston Turville. 82t Michael Dixon, Dover. 82b Ekdotike Athenon, S.A., Athens. 84bl Giraudon, Paris. 84br Tretyakov Gallery, Moscow. 86–87 KM. 88, 90 Werner Forman Archive. 91 KM.

List of Abbreviations
BM British Museum. CF Chris Forsey. KM Kevin Maddison.

Quote from *The Canterbury Tales* by Geoffrey Chaucer taken from translation by Nevill Coghill (Penguin Classics, Revised Edition 1977), Copyright 1951 by Nevill Coghill, copyright © Nevill Coghill, 1958, 1960, 1975, 1977.

Contents

Introduction   4

Timelines   6

Europe   8

PART ONE:
A HISTORY OF MEDIEVAL EUROPE

Europe 350–1500 C.E.   12

The Barbarian Movements   14

The Empire of Justinian   16

Ravenna   18

Carolingian Europe   20

Sutton Hoo   22

Viking Expansion   24

The Byzantine Empire   26

The Plantagenet Empire   28

The Bayeux Tapestry   30

Domesday Book   32

The Crusades   34

The German Empire   36

The Medieval Church   38

Education   40

Cathedral-building   42

Stories in Stained Glass   44

Medieval Arts and Crafts   46

Science, Medicine, and Printing   48

PART TWO:
THE LANDS OF MEDIEVAL EUROPE

Travel   52

France   54

France · Sites   58

Italy   60

Italy · Sites   62

Trade   64

The British Isles   66

Castles   68

The Countryside   70

Spain and Portugal   72

Mapmaking   74

Journey to Compostela   76

Central Europe   78

Everyday Life   80

Southeastern Europe   82

Northeastern Europe   84

A Russian Village   86

Scandinavia   88

Scandinavia · Sites   90

Glossary   92

Further Reading/Web Sites   92

Gazetteer   93

Index   95

Introduction

THIS IS A BOOK ABOUT THE PEOPLES OF MEDIEVAL EUROPE. BUT what does the word "medieval" mean? It comes from two Latin words meaning "middle age." In fact, many writers still call this period of history the Middle Ages, hence the title of our book. What were they in the middle of? The medieval age begins at the end of the Roman period in western Europe, in about 350 C.E. It ends with the discovery—by Europeans—of the world beyond Europe in the late 15th century.

We started by talking about "peoples" of medieval Europe. In this book you will read about a number of different peoples over a period that covers more than 1,000 years. Some of these peoples were relatively small in number but have had great influence on later periods. The Vikings were such a people. No huge armies of Vikings sailed from their homelands of Scandinavia, but their influence can still be seen today in towns and settlements across northern Europe and beyond to Iceland, Greenland, and even North America.

Because there were a number of peoples looking for new lands or just eager for power, the boundaries between countries frequently changed. Here you will be able to read about, and follow on the maps, at least part of the story of each "country" in medieval Europe. Some of them became "world powers," as we say today.

Part of the story of medieval Europe is the struggle between these world powers. For example, there were wars between Christians and the followers of the prophet Muhammad, whose religion is Islam—the Muslim peoples. You will probably already have read about the Crusades to win back the Holy Land (Palestine), but there were other struggles going on. There was also a conflict between different types of Christian worship.

How do we discover the evidence for the peoples of medieval Europe? As for all historic periods, there are two main sources. Documents give us one form of evidence that can be read. Archaeological evidence is the physical remains of the past—perhaps a leather shoe preserved in a well, or a great cathedral still in use today. These two very different types of evidence together help build up the picture that we have of the past.

The book is divided into two main sections. The first, **A History of Medieval Europe**, looks at the development of the most important empires that set the boundaries in the past. The second section, **The Lands of Medieval Europe**, examines in greater detail the individual countries that we can all recognize today and their own histories.

The Middle Ages is an atlas so there are lots of maps to help you understand the development of Europe. As you read through the book, compare the various regions with the map of Europe today on pages 8 and 9 to see how different medieval Europe really was—the past is a foreign country!

But there is much more to this book than just maps. In both sections you will find special features that look at life in medieval times and at some of the remains that you can see today. Our story is arranged in double-page spreads, so you can read the book from beginning to end, or just dip into it to learn about a specific topic. The Glossary on page 92 contains definitions of historical terms used in the book.

Abbreviations used in this book
B.C.E. = Before Common Era (also known as B.C.).
C.E. = Common Era (also known as A.D.). c. = *circa* (about).
in = inch; ft = foot; mi = mile.
cm = centimeter; m = meter; km = kilometer.

▶ The town of Cordes, in the Tarn region of France, founded in 1222.

Timelines

	400	500	600	700	800
ARTS AND ARCHITECTURE		Christian churches built in Rome, Jerusalem, Constantinople	532–37 Santa Sophia, Constantinople c.550 Ravenna mosaics	c.650 Sutton Hoo ship burial c.698 Lindisfarne Gospels	735–804 Alcuin, scholar	c.870 *Codex Aure* illustrated manuscrip
CHRISTIAN CHURCH	313 Edict of Milan granting toleration to Christians		526 death of St. Benedict 560 Irish missions to continent 590–604 Gregory I pope			817 Benedict of Aniane reforms monasteries 860 Cyril and Methodi sent to Moravia
ROMAN EMPIRE	395 division of the Empire	430 death of Augustine at Hippo Regius 451 Council of Chaceldon	533 Africa restored to Roman Empire	610–41 Heraclius emperor	716–17 Muslim siege of Constantinople 717–41 Leo III emperor 730–843 iconoclasm	867–86 Basil I, first emperor of Macedon dynasty
ISLAM				622 Muhammad goes to Medina 661–80 Muawiya, first Umayyad caliph at Damascus	762 foundation of Baghdad as Abbasid capital	909 foundation of Fatir caliphate in north Africa
SPAIN		409 Vandals, Alans, and Suevi enter Spain	509 Visigoths defeated at Vouillé and fall back on Spain		711 Muslims invade Spain	c.860 serious Viking assaults on Spain
FRANCE		486 Clovis defeats Syagrius	c.507 conversion of Clovis to Catholicism	687 Pepin of Austrasia defeats Neustrians at Tertry	732 Charles Martel defeats Saracens at Poitiers 751 Pepin III becomes king of the Franks	888 Odo count of Paris becomes king
ITALY		476 Odovacar king of Italy	536 Belisarius reconquers Rome 568 Lombard invasion of Italy	668 Constans II killed at Syracuse	774 Charlemagne becomes king of Italy	
GERMANY	341 Ulfila begins conversion of Goths 376 Goths cross the Danube	406 Germans cross the Rhine			772–804 Saxon wars	800 Charlemagne crowned emperor 843 Treaty of Verdun: empire divided
EASTERN EUROPE			Slavs begin to infiltrate Balkans			864 conversion of Bulgars
BRITAIN AND IRELAND			563 St. Columba in Iona 597 Roman mission to England	664 Synod of Whitby	Mercian supremacy 731 Bede completes *Ecclesiastical History* 793 first Viking raids	836 Danes established at Dublin 899 death of Alfred Wessex king of Engla
SCANDINAVIA						860 Danes established Iceland

Diocletian and Maximian, c.300.

Santa Sophia, Constantinople, 532–37.

The emperor Charlemagne, crowned 800.

900	1000	1100	1200	1300	1400

c.985 *Beowulf*

Viking ship, Oseberg, 10th century.

c.1063 San Marco, Venice

The Tower of London, c.1080.

1194–1220 Chartres Cathedral built

Sculptures from Chartres Cathedral, 1134–50.

c.1225–74 Aquinas
1265–1321 Dante
1266–1337 Giotto

The town hall, Siena, 1297–1376.

1304–74 Petrarch
1345–1400 Chaucer
1377–1446 Brunelleschi
1386–1466 Donatello
c.1390–1441 van Eyck

c.1400–74 Dufay
1452–1519 Leonardo da Vinci
1471–1528 Dürer

David by Donatello, 1430.

900	1000	1100	1200	1300	1400
911 foundation of Cluny	1046 Synod of Sutri—beginning of reform in Roman church	1115 foundation of Clairvaux 1179 Lateran Council III	1209 Franciscan order approved 1215 Paris university receives first statutes	c.1309–77 Pope's residence at Avignon 1378 schism begins	1415–17 Council of Constance
963–69 Nicephorus Phocas emperor	1018 final defeat of Bulgars 1071 battle of Manzikert	1176 Manuel I defeated by Seljuksat Myriokephalon	1204 Fourth Crusade; capture of Constantinople 1261 restoration of empire		1453 capture of Constantinople
	1055 Seljuks capture Baghdad 1071 Manzikert Seljuks occupy Asia Minor 1095 First Crusade	1171 Saladin conquers Fatimid Egypt 1187 Saladin recaptures Jerusalem	1218–21 Fifth Crusade 1250–1517 Mamluk dynasty in Egypt	1326 Ottomans take Bursa 1389 Ottomans defeat Serbs at Kosovo	1402 death of Timur the Lame 1453 Muslims capture Constantinople
929 Umayyad caliphate in Spain	1031 end of Cordoban caliphate 1085 Christians capture Toledo	1137 count of Barcelona becomes king of Aragon 1147 Lisbon captured from Muslims	1235–48 Catholics conquer Cordoba and Seville	1369 Trastamara dynasty in Castile	1479 Ferdinand V marries Isabella of Castile 1492 Discovery of "New World" 1498 Vasco da Gama reaches India
911 Rollo installed in Normandy 987 Hugh, first Capetian king of the Franks			1210–29 Albigensian wars 1226–70 Louis IX 1284 war between England and France	1337 war begins between Philip VI of Valois and Edward III	1431 Joan of Arc burned 1477 death of Charles the Rash, last Valois duke of Burgundy
962 Otto I crowned emperor	1030 Normans established at Aversa	1130–54 Roger II king of Sicily	1212–50 Frederick II emperor and king of Sicily 1252 first florins struck in Florence	1347 plague reaches Genoa from Crimea 1385 Gian Galeazzo unites Visconti lands	1434 Cosimo de Medici returns to Florence 1454 Peace of Lodi
955 Otto I defeats Magyars at the Lech		1122 Concordat of Worms 1159–77 imperial–papal quarrel	1273 Rudolf of Hapsburg elected king of the Romans 1291 first Swiss alliance	1338 Declaration of Rense 1348 university founded at Prague	1419–36 Hussite wars
966 foundation of Poland 989 Vladimir of Kiev becomes Christian	1000 Otto III founds archdiocese at Gniezno 1001 kingdom of Hungary established		1241 Mongols defeat Christians at Legnica	1320 Polish kingdom reunited 1386 Poland ruled with Lithuania	1478 Ivan III takes Novgorod
973 first recorded coronation of an English king	1017 Canute becomes king of England 1066 Norman conquest 1086 Domesday Book	1154 Henry II first Angevin king of England	1215 Magna Carta 1284 English king establishes rule over Wales 1296 war with Scotland	1381 peasants' revolt	1483 Henry Tudor made king
995–c.1000 Olaf I king of Norway		1104 archbishopric of Lund founded		1397 Norway, Sweden, and Denmark united by Kalmar Union	

Europe

WHAT DO YOU UNDERSTAND BY THE word "Europe"? Perhaps it will depend on where you live—whether your home is in Europe or in one of the other six continents, the great landmasses that make up our world. For you, Europe might be a place you go to on vacation or a place where you can see and wonder at the great monuments of the past.

Europe today

One way to define Europe could be as all the countries north of the Mediterranean and Black Seas, from Iceland and Portugal east to Turkey and the Russian border. Another way could be as the European Union (EU). In 2004 the EU expanded to include 25 member states: Austria, Belgium, Cyprus, Czech Republic, Denmark, Estonia, Finland, France, Germany, Greece, Hungary, Ireland, Italy, Latvia, Lithuania, Luxembourg, Malta, the Netherlands, Poland, Portugal, Slovakia, Slovenia, Spain, Sweden and the United Kingdom. Bulgaria and Romania joined in 2007, and others are poised to join it in the near future.

The physical shape of Europe

Yet another way of defining Europe is to look at the physical boundaries, especially those between the continents of Europe and Asia. These boundaries are the mountain ranges of the Caucasus (between the Black Sea and the Caspian Sea) and the Urals (in Russia), both just off our map to the east.

Medieval Europe

The definition of Europe we use in this book about the medieval period is quite different. It has to be. We must start with what the Romans thought of as their Empire—and add to it as necessary. We must add countries and areas at different times in the medieval period. To the question "What exactly is Europe?" a Roman would not have been able to give a reply. An educated person from medieval Europe, however, would have known what the question meant and been able to respond.

▶ This map shows the modern boundaries of the Europe you are going to read about in this book. You will see that these boundaries are often quite different from those in the medieval period. The physical features are important. Mountain ranges, seas, deserts, and rivers usually defined where people lived and where they could travel to.

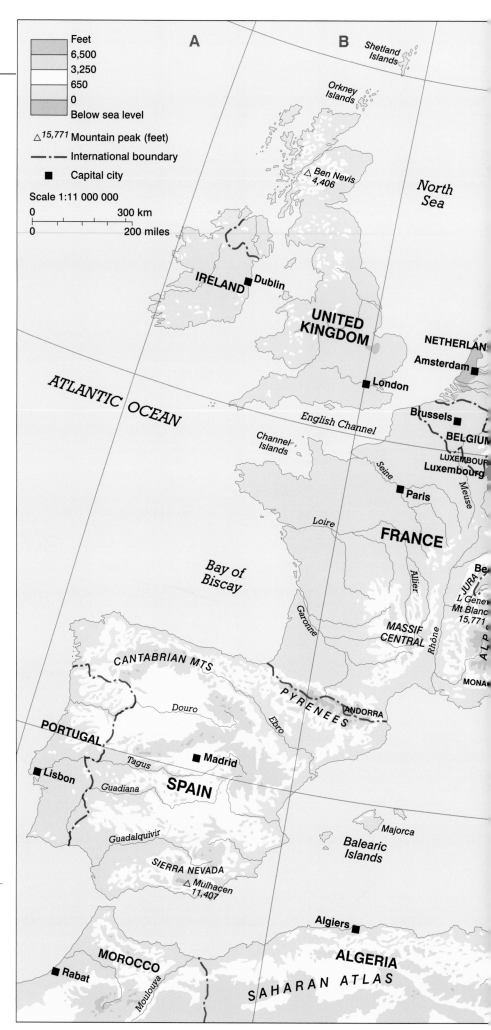

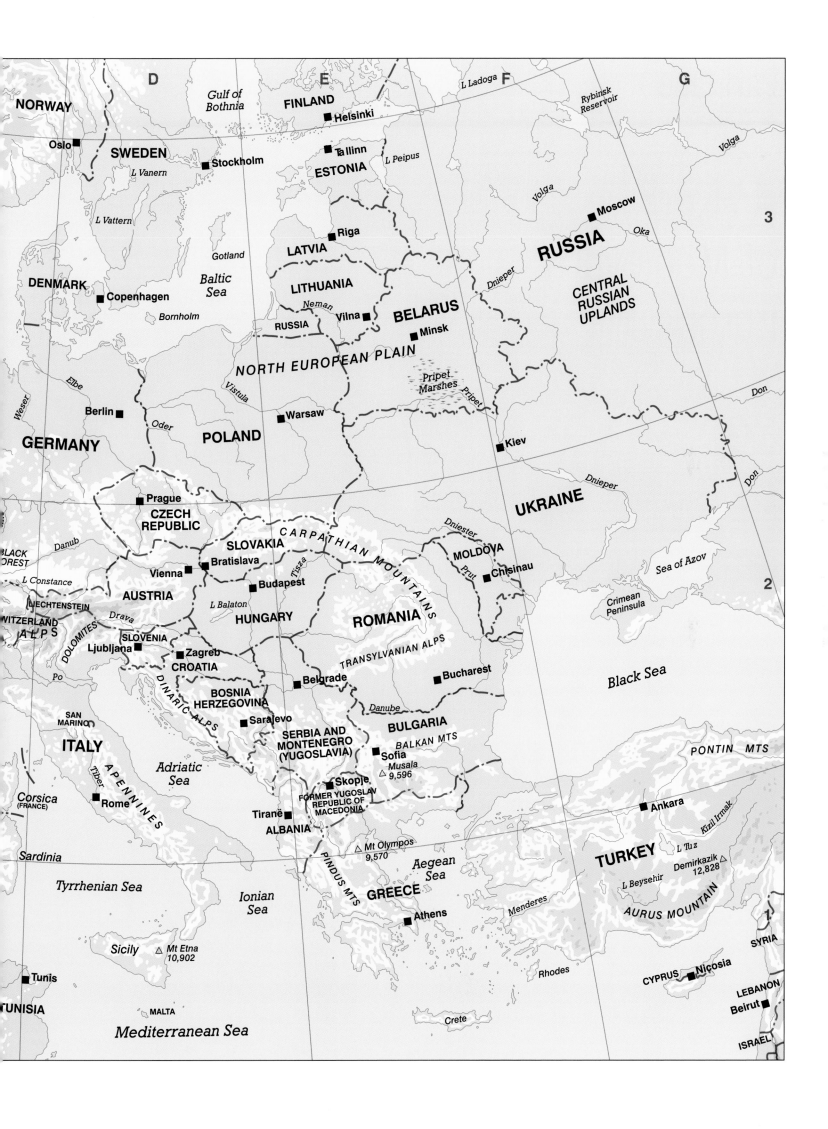

Part One

A History of Medieval Europe

▲ A 10th-century ivory bookcover showing Pope Gregory the Great at his writing desk.

▶ Detail from an early medieval illuminated manuscript, the Lindisfarne Gospels. Lindisfarne Island, off the northeast coast of England, was a focal point of English Christianity from 635 C.E. to about 950 C.E.

Europe 350–1500 C.E.

Roman Empire
Diocletianic diocese boundary
East-west division of Empire, 395
Territorial boundary
● Important settlement

Scale 1 : 24 000 000

| 0 | | 600 km |
| 0 | | 400 miles |

North Sea

Baltic Sea

BRITAIN
●Londinium

ATLANTIC OCEAN

Colonia Agrippina
Rhine
Lutetia
Loire
GAUL
Caesarodunum
Danube
PANNONIA
Burdigala
Lugdunum
Aquileia
VIENNENSIS ●Vienna
Sirmium
WEST ROMAN EMPIRE
Ravenna
Black Sea
SPAIN
Narbonne
ITALY
MOESIA
THRACE
Tagus
Toletum
Corsica
Rome
Constantinople
●Emerita Augusta
Sardinia
Thessalonica
Ancyra ●
PONTUS
Balearic Is
EAST ROMAN EMPIRE
Amida
●Carthago Nova
Sicily
Smyrna
ASIA
Athens
●Antioch
Carthage
Cyprus
ORIENS
AFRICA
Mediterranean Sea
Crete
Jerusalem

◄ Europe in 350.
For centuries the Romans had increased the size of the lands they controlled. At its biggest there were probably as many as 60 million people living in the Roman Empire. It was always difficult to control parts of this great Empire, especially those provinces that were furthest away from the center of power.

Diocletian (made Roman emperor in 284) split the huge Empire into two. He ruled from the east and appointed Maximian to rule in the west. To organize and control this empire, he divided it into 12 dioceses—marked on the map. After Emperor Theodosius died in 395, the Empire was ruled separately in the east and the west.

Frankish Empire
Frontier land (march)
East Roman Empire
Muslim land
Territorial boundary
Picts Name of people
● Important settlement

Scale 1 : 24 000 000

| 0 | | 600 km |
| 0 | | 400 miles |

Scots Picts
North Sea
Baltic Sea
NORTHUMBRIA
Danes
Welsh MERCIA
WESSEX ●London
Cologne
Rhine
ATLANTIC OCEAN
●Paris
Metz
Loire
Regensburg
Danube
FRANKISH EMPIRE
PANNONIA
Poitiers ●
Lyon
Venice
BULGAR KHANATE
Oviedo
Milan
Slavs
●Belgrade
GALICIA
Ravenna
Black Sea
SPANISH MARCH
Narbonne
PAPAL STATE
Trebizond
Tagus
Corsica
DUCHY OF BENEVENTO
Durazzo
Toledo
Barcelona
Rome
Constantinople
Lisbon
UMAYYAD EMIRATE
Valencia
Benevento
Thessalonica
●Ancyra
Sardinia
EAST ROMAN EMPIRE
Balearic Is
●Almería
Sicily
Smyrna
●Tangier
Athens
●Antioch
IDRISID CALIPHATE
AGHLABID EMIRATE
Mediterranean Sea
Cyprus
ABBASID CALIPHATE
Crete
Jerusalem

◄ Europe in 800.
The Romans called those who lived beyond their boundaries, who did not speak Latin or live the Roman way of life, *barbari*. By 800 the West Empire had broken down and several "barbarian" states had been founded.

The East Roman (Byzantine) Empire based in Constantinople kept its influence in the east, in southern Italy and Sardinia. Other parts of the old Empire in the west were ruled by the Franks and the Muslims (followers of the Islamic religion) who dominated North Africa and the Mediterranean.

The Frankish Empire under Charlemagne was Christian and tried to revive Roman traditions. But by Roman standards even the Franks were barbarians.

► Europe in 1150.
By the 12th century Roman provinces that the Muslims had gained from the East Roman Empire were won back. Crusading Christians from the west had established Crusader states in the Holy Land, though they were under threat from the Muslims.

In the west, Christians had recovered parts of southern Spain and Italy. The Holy Roman (or German) Empire created by the Franks had strengthened its hold on Germany and Italy and had begun to expand eastward into the territory of the Slavs.

At this time it looked as if a new Christian empire would expand to control as large an area as the Romans had once conquered.

► Europe in 1500.
By 1500 great changes had taken place. Any hope that a Christian empire might be established throughout the Mediterranean region was crushed by the success of a new empire—that of the Ottomans.

The East Roman Empire had been overrun by Ottoman Turks. Constantinople itself was captured in 1453. The eastern Empire could no longer be called Christian. The Holy Land, once protected by western Christians, passed into the hands of the Muslims.

In the west several smaller kingdoms were established and powerful rulers fought with each other for control of territories. Nations were being created, often out of a number of different peoples.

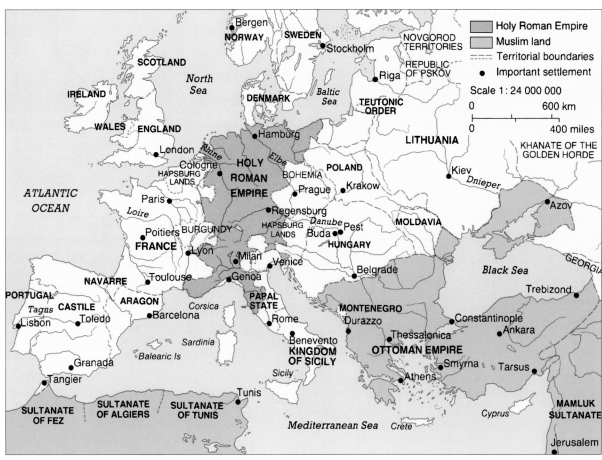

13

The Barbarian Movements

"The army of the Visigoths led by Athaulph marched on Gaul ... The Romans were no longer able to win back Britain—from now on it continued to be ruled by whoever had seized power."

THE YEAR BEING DESCRIBED IS 411. THE writer is Procopius, a civil servant who was born about 500 and wrote, among other works, histories of the wars of the Roman emperor Justinian. We have seen (page 12) that the Romans, in their vast Empire had suffered from those peoples they called "barbarians." Not all these enemies were uneducated and murderous, however. They often wanted to rule their own countries and to break away from Rome.

From the northwest

From the countries to the north of the Rhine River tribes called Saxons, Angles, and Jutes invaded southern Britain. At first they settled alongside Romano-British communities in the eastern part of the country. Like many other barbarians, some were

▼ Unsettled conditions in eastern Britain meant that many people chose to bury their wealth for safekeeping. The scene below depicts the burial of the so-called Thetford treasure. This was a hoard of fourth-century gold and silver objects, probably buried by a merchant, from Thetford in Norfolk. It was discovered by chance in 1979 and is now in the British Museum, London.

signed up as paid "mercenary" soldiers. Britain was unsettled, however, and many people fled to other parts of the country. Hoards of coins and valuables they hid have been discovered.

Terror from the east

"A report spread that the Goths had suddenly descended like a whirlwind from the high mountains and were ravaging and destroying everything in their path."

The historian Ammianus Marcellinus, writing in the fourth century, summed up the Romans' fear of the hordes of invaders. The Goths came from the steppes of Russia. There were two groups—Visigoths and Ostrogoths. Roman emperors paid some of them to stay out of Roman territory and persuaded some to move farther west (to Italy and into Gaul). Despite this, they were unstoppable, and they began to take over huge areas that had once been Roman. Rome itself was plundered by the Visigoths in 410.

▲ This gold belt buckle from the Thetford treasure has a hinged bow in the form of two facing horses' heads. The high quality of the metalworking and the style of the figure suggest that it was made in the late fourth century.

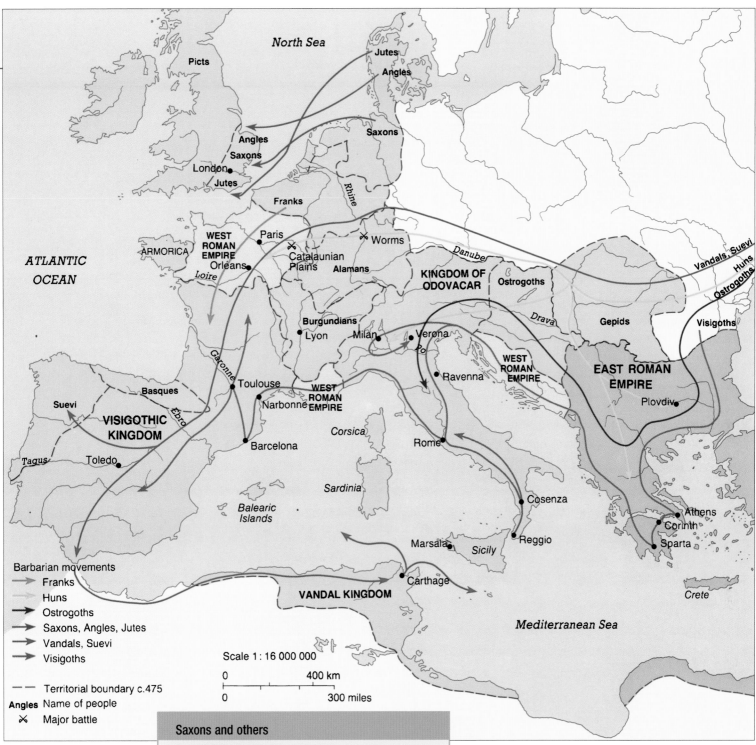

Barbarian movements
→ Franks
→ Huns
→ Ostrogoths
→ Saxons, Angles, Jutes
→ Vandals, Suevi
→ Visigoths

--- Territorial boundary c.475
Angles Name of people
✕ Major battle

Scale 1 : 16 000 000

| 0 | 400 km |
| 0 | 300 miles |

▲ Migrations of barbarians in the fourth and fifth centuries. There were many reasons for the movement of peoples from outside the Roman world and inside its boundaries. Some were looking for new farmland, but others enjoyed waging war.

Saxons and others

By mid-fifth century Saxons, Angles, and Jutes have begun to settle in Britain permanently.

410 In Italy, Rome taken by Visigoth chief Alaric.

493 Ravenna falls to Theodoric, king of the Ostrogoths. Theodoric dies fighting with the Romans against the Huns in 526.

West Roman Empire: 414 Visigoths take over Narbonne but abandon the town in 415.

436 Burgundians defeated by Huns at Worms.

451 Attila the Hun defeated by Roman general Aetius with help from barbarian troops at Catalaunian Plains.
486 Franks take over territory in West Roman Empire.

East Roman Empire: 382 Emperor Theodosius allows Visigoths to settle on the northern edge of the Empire.

468 Failure of Emperor Leo's expedition against Vandals.

Barbarians were human, too ...

Despite their reputation, the barbarians had their good side. It is true that they did not live a Roman way of life and left hardly any written record of themselves, but some, like the Goths, were Christians. Theodoric, king of the Ostrogoths, was Christian and well educated. In his capital, Ravenna in Italy, he built a number of important buildings, including churches, in the Roman style.

The Ostrogoths and other barbarians employed skilled metalworkers and jewelers to produce elaborate crowns, crosses, and bookcovers. They liked to wear jewelry on their clothes.

The Empire of Justinian

THE ROMAN EMPIRE IN THE EAST WAS STILL ruled by emperors at the end the fifth century. But the situation in the West Empire was quite different. There, army commanders usually appointed emperors. In 476 Ordovacar, king of a group of German tribes who had settled in Italy, decided to rule instead of the emperor Romulus Augustulus. He advanced on Ravenna and deposed the emperor, although he spared him his life.

Reoccupying the West

It was not until the reign of Justinian as Emperor in the east that the West Empire was brought under Roman control again. After he came to power in 527, Justinian's first move against the barbarians who had taken over the Empire was in North Africa. Vandals, originally from central Europe, had swept westward through Spain and into Africa early in the fifth century. Although the Vandals had set up a strong kingdom there, Justinian's campaign won back North Africa in a few months in 533 and resulted in the end of the Vandal empire.

Generals Belisarius and Narses

The emperor's two commanders attacked Italy from different directions. Belisarius occupied Sicily, Sardinia, and Corsica, and then moved into mainland Italy, finally reoccupying Rome in 536. After a century of fear, Rome was now freed from Vandal power in the Mediterranean.

Narses moved across land to lay siege to Ravenna in 540. Ravenna had become the official residence of the barbarian rulers of Italy—the Ostrogoth Theodoric, for example. There was some resistance to the reoccupation by Roman forces, but this was finally crushed in 552. Narses ruled the west, which by then included a small part of Spain, from Ravenna as the emperor Justinian's chosen governor.

◀ This portrait of the emperor Justinian is a small part of a large mosaic picture in the church of San Vitale, Ravenna, Italy. The building was begun by the king of the Ostrogoths, Theodoric, in about 520. Justinian had the church decorated with wall and ceiling mosaics in about 550.

▶ The reconquests of Justinian. Compare this map of the countries around the Mediterranean with the one on the previous page. For a short period, at least, Roman authority was reestablished in the west by Justinian. Roman trade could now begin again across the Mediterranean.

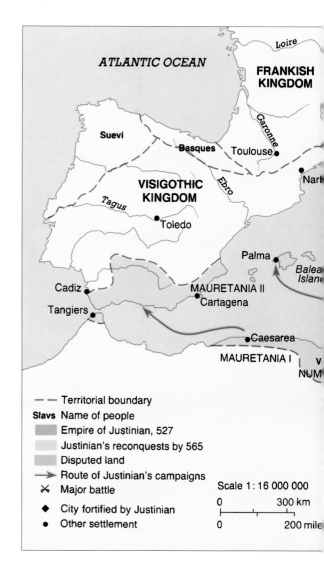

- - - Territorial boundary
Slavs Name of people
▨ Empire of Justinian, 527
▨ Justinian's reconquests by 565
▨ Disputed land
→ Route of Justinian's campaigns
✕ Major battle
◆ City fortified by Justinian
● Other settlement

Scale 1 : 16 000 000

0   300 km

0   200 mile

After Justinian

Justinian died in 565. Italy was invaded by the Lombards in 568, but they were not able to take over the whole country. Only in the late seventh century were Africa and then Spain taken over by the Muslims. The East Roman Empire, which was also known as the Byzantine Empire, continued to be ruled by emperors until 1453 when its capital, Constantinople, fell to the Ottoman Turks.

Events of Justinian's reign

527 Justinian proclaimed emperor with his wife Theodora.

533 Campaigns against barbarians in Africa and Italy.

535–54 Ostrogoths conquered in Italy.

552 Reoccupation of southern Spain.

Attacks from outside Empire: Slavs **534, 547, 549, 551**. Bulgars **534, 538**. Huns **539–40, 559**. Persian Emperor Khusrau I makes frequent attacks until peace treaty in **561**.

565 Emperor Justinian dies.

▲ Part of the helmet of Agilulf, king of the Lombards from 590 to 615. Although the Lombards invaded Italy after Justinian's time, the decoration shows Agilulf (center with pointed beard) guarded by his warriors wearing Roman armor.

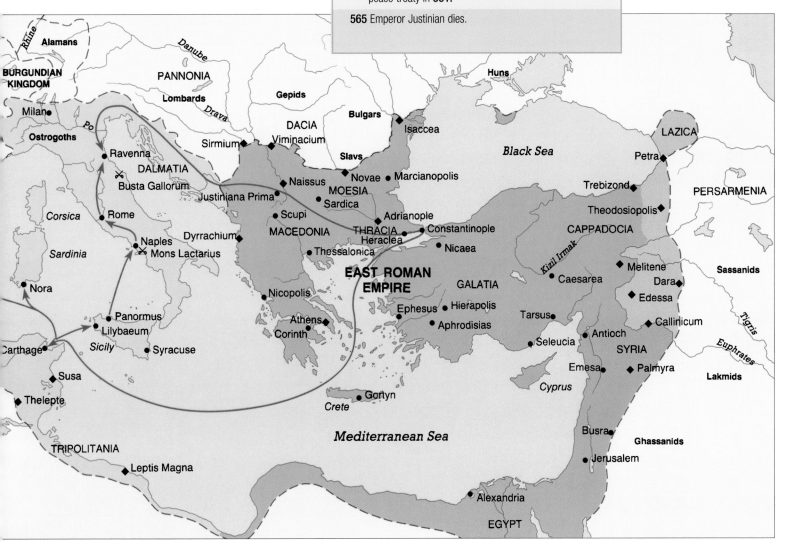

Ravenna

RAVENNA, A PORT IN NORTHEASTERN Italy, was enlarged in 23 C.E. by the first Roman emperor, Augustus, who based his northern navy there. The city became much more important after 402, when it was chosen as the official residence of the Roman emperors of the west so that they could have close links with the emperors in the east in Constantinople.

Imperial buildings

Buildings in Ravenna had to be splendid enough for the court of the Roman emperor. One that survives today and that greatly influenced the design of later buildings was the church of Sacra Croce (the Sacred Cross). It was built in about 425 at the command of the empress Galla Placidia, who was the mother of the emperor Valentinian III.

Attached to the church was a mausoleum (a building for burial) with beautiful mosaics on its domed ceiling. They show a deep sparkling blue heaven with gold stars shining through.

Christian conquerors

In 493 Ravenna was captured by the Ostrogoth king Theodoric. He governed Italy from here with the help of Roman advisers. He had lived from the ages of eight to 18 in the imperial court at Constantinople. He was, therefore, a well-educated man. During his 30-year reign in Ravenna he put up a number of fine buildings and adapted or changed others. Many of these buildings were Christian churches.

Regained by Justinian

The Roman emperor in the east, Justinian, sent his forces to drive out the Goths from Italy. After Theodoric's death in 526, Ravenna remained an important city. Justinian ordered new buildings to be put up and others to be adapted—as he did elsewhere in the empire.

In Ravenna the most important building was the church of San Vitale, one of the finest examples of Byzantine architecture in western Europe. The church was begun by Bishop Ecclesius of Ravenna under the Ostrogothic queen Amalasuntha but was completed by Justinian. It was the official church of the imperial court, built of long thin bricks but with marble columns inside and decorated with splendid mosaics on its upper walls and domed ceilings. One mosaic is a picture of Justinian and Theodora bringing gifts to the holy altar.

▶ This beautiful mosaic dome was commissioned by King Theodoric in Ravenna. It shows Christ being baptized in the Jordan River by John the Baptist (on Christ's left). Above Christ's head can be seen a cross on a cushion. You will need to look at the mosaic closely or with a magnifying glass to see the little pieces of stone that make up the picture.

▼ Mosaics—pictures and patterns mainly in stone— were made by both Greek and Roman artists. Rich Romans, especially in southern Italy in places such as Pompeii, used Greek mosaic-makers to construct fine floor and wall pictures.

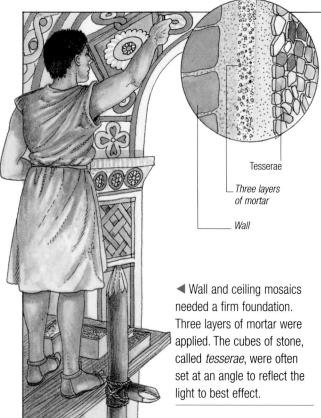

Tesserae

Three layers of mortar

Wall

◀ Wall and ceiling mosaics needed a firm foundation. Three layers of mortar were applied. The cubes of stone, called *tesserae*, were often set at an angle to reflect the light to best effect.

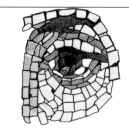

◀ Empress Theodora on a mosaic in the church of San Vitale. Above, her eyes are made of bits of stone.

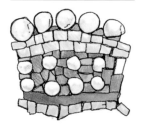

▲ The mosaic-maker used mother-of-pearl for the empress's headdress to make it look real.

Carolingian Europe

WHEN OSTROGOTHS RULED ITALY AND Visigoths ruled Spain in the sixth century, the countries we now know as France, Switzerland, Germany, Luxembourg, Belgium, and the Netherlands were ruled by a number of different Christian kings. The most powerful rulers were the Franks. They were right on the edge of the Christian world and fought against non-Christian peoples beyond (the Frisians and Saxons). They also established many monasteries in their lands.

The Frankish kingdom of Clovis was later divided into three parts: Austrasia, Neustria, and Burgundy. One of these kingdoms, Austrasia (present-day Germany), became powerful not only because its people were warlike but also because they controlled the main route between the newly established Christian communities in England and Rome itself. Pilgrims and monks had to go through Austrasia and across the Alps into Italy, as the route through southern Gaul (now France) was blocked by the Saracen Muslims.

The Carolingian family

Charles Martel was the first of the Carolingian family to gain a reputation in Europe—his name means Charles the Hammer. He defeated the Saracen Muslims at Poitiers (in western France) in 732. He made himself the most powerful ruler in the whole of Gaul. His son, Pepin III, won back lost territories and conquered new lands. He was the first of the family to become king of all the Franks.

By Pepin III's death in 768, the Frankish Empire stretched from the borders of Spain north to the Netherlands, and east from the edge of Brittany (in western France) to Bohemia.

Charles the Great—Charlemagne

Pepin's two sons inherited his lands. When the younger son died in 771, the elder, Charles, became sole ruler. This Charles was called, in Latin, Carolus Magnus, or Charles the Great—Charlemagne. The word Carolingian comes from his name Carolus. Charlemagne reigned as emperor for more than 45 years and increased the size of the Empire. He organized about 60 military campaigns—leading half of them himself. His wars against the Saxons were long, drawn-out, and brutal.

By the end of the eighth century the boundaries of the Carolingian Empire had moved north to take over the Saxon lands, south into Italy and east into Bavaria. The pope in Rome recognized the considerable authority of Charlemagne and crowned him Emperor of the West. After Charlemagne's death in 814, his Empire continued to be governed by his only surviving son, Louis, at least for a time.

Charlemagne's world

Charlemagne had no capital city but in later years he often ruled his huge empire from his palace in Aachen, Germany. He was a ruler with a great interest in education and culture. Besides his own Frankish language he also spoke Latin. He understood Greek, but never learned to write it.

Both in Charlemagne's time and during the reigns of later Carolingian kings, monks were encouraged to study manuscripts that had survived from the Roman and Greek worlds and to make new copies of them. It is because of this that we are now able to read the "classics." The monks also copied the Bible and other sacred writings, and the manuscripts that survive from this time are among the most clear and legible documents in the history of writing.

▲ A bronze statue of Charlemagne from Metz.

▶ The back cover of the Lindau Gospels was decorated with gold, silver-gilt, and enamel in Charlemagne's time. The decoration of the intertwining animals is earlier.

◀ ▲ Impressive religious buildings and objects show how important Christian worship was at this time. Left, the Carolingian church of a monastery at Corvey in northern Germany. Above, a ninth-century enamel cross, now in the Vatican.

Sutton Hoo

IN 1938 THE OWNER OF SOME LARGE barrows (mounds of earth) in Suffolk, England, wanted to find out what was inside. She asked the local museum to find her an excavator. The next year one of the most spectacular archaeological discoveries of the century was made.

The burial of a king

Inside the largest of the barrows archaeologists found a grave containing the traces of a wooden boat 89 feet (27 m) long. Although the body had rotted away, it had once been surrounded by many beautiful and priceless objects. The archaeologists believed that this was the grave of an East Anglian king called Raedwald who died in about 625. Raedwald was also declared *Bretwalda*, or High King, of Britain from about 616. Although the type of burial was pagan (not Christian), Raedwald was buried with some Christian objects. Possibly, he had converted to the Christian religion.

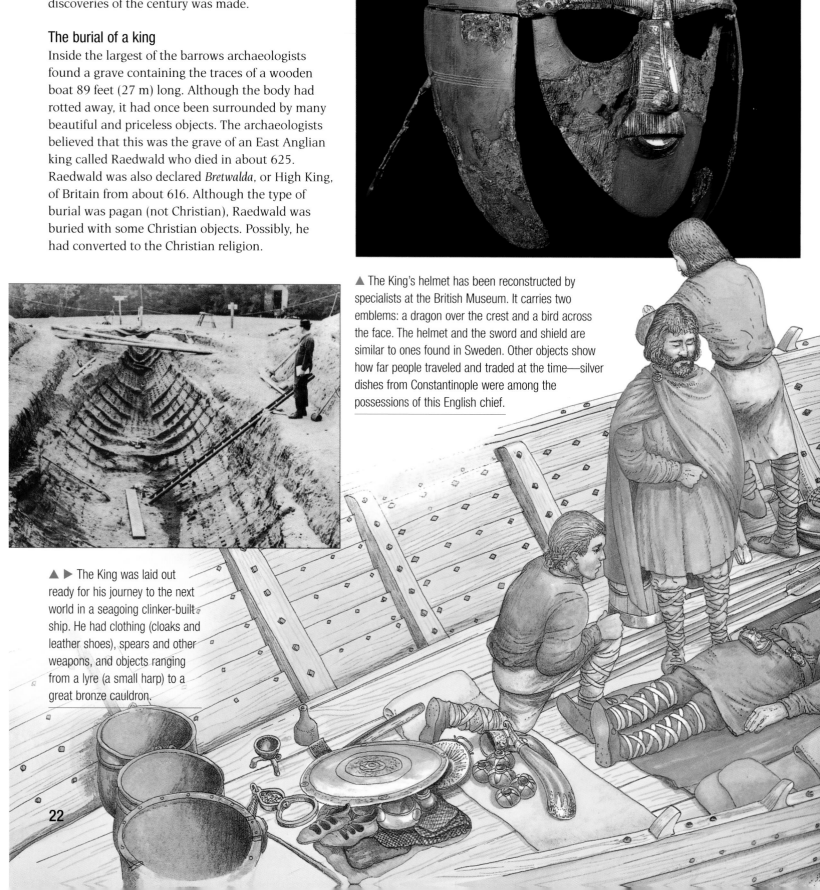

▲ The King's helmet has been reconstructed by specialists at the British Museum. It carries two emblems: a dragon over the crest and a bird across the face. The helmet and the sword and shield are similar to ones found in Sweden. Other objects show how far people traveled and traded at the time—silver dishes from Constantinople were among the possessions of this English chief.

▲ ▶ The King was laid out ready for his journey to the next world in a seagoing clinker-built ship. He had clothing (cloaks and leather shoes), spears and other weapons, and objects ranging from a lyre (a small harp) to a great bronze cauldron.

Viking Expansion

"The ravaging of heathens destroyed God's church at Lindisfarne, with much plunder and slaughter."

THE VIKINGS (THE "HEATHENS" WRITTEN about above) were robbers who came by sea—in other words, pirates. This quotation is from the *Anglo-Saxon Chronicle*, a history of England put together in the ninth century. This entry is for 793. Many people had every reason to be frightened of these "wolves to be feared" as their warships sailed from their homelands in Scandinavia.

Vikings at home
Vikings were, in fact, several different peoples who lived in what we now know as Norway, Sweden, and Denmark. Many people think of them today simply as warlike raiders. But not all Vikings were like that. They included farmers, great traders, and town builders. Their artists and craftspeople produced many beautiful objects.

The search for new lands
Many Vikings set off from their homelands in search of new lands to settle and farm, such as Iceland. Other voyages were carried out for plunder first, then for settlement. Norwegian Vikings began to settle in the islands off the north coast of Scotland at the beginning of the eighth century. From there they moved down the west coast of Britain and across the sea to Ireland.

The Danish Vikings plundered Lindisfarne on the northeast coast of Britain and later traveled farther south to East Anglia. Vikings from Sweden moved across the Baltic Sea into eastern Europe. Traveling by river, they eventually reached Constantinople, attacking it in 860.

By the ninth century Viking merchant-warriors had built up a large trading network across the Baltic Sea, linking Europe from end to end.

Plunder, slaves, and trade
The Viking raiders certainly looked for and collected plunder but they also required slaves—they called them *thralls*. Some peoples they attacked were forced to buy them off with gold. Trade was important, too. For example, a Viking prince established a trading contract by force with Constantinople in 907. The Vikings supplied slaves, timber, furs, and honey in exchange for gold, silver, and luxury goods. Before coins were used, the Vikings chopped up silver objects (often jewelry) and used them for exchange.

Ships and the sea
The Vikings were great shipbuilders and sailors. This was the key to their success as traders, raiders, and settlers. They made very long voyages in fast ships, even crossing from Iceland to Greenland to settle in North America. Their ships, built with overlapping timber planks, were powered by sails and oars and had grand names such as "Sea-striding Bison" and "Long Serpent." The Vikings built not only "longships" for raiding (each one holding up to 200 warriors) but also wider trading ships called *knarrs* and little rowing boats called *faerings*.

▲ Reconstruction of a ship excavated from a royal burial mound at Oseberg near Oslo in Norway.

▼ Across the Atlantic. The search for new lands and an escape from murderous feuds took some Vikings farther overseas. By about 1000 they had built settlements in Labrador and Newfoundland.

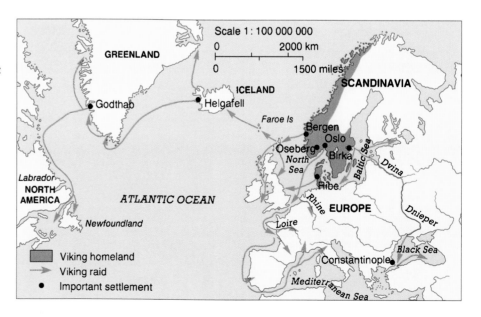

▲ A drawing of a Viking farmhouse at Stöng in Iceland, based on archaeological excavations. Viking settlements here were destroyed by a volcanic eruption in 1104. The farm buildings were made of turf and consisted of hall, living room, dairy, and bathroom.

▼ Viking settlements in Iceland and Greenland. Sheep farming was the basis of the Vikings' new northern settlements. Written records show the settlers as hardy and sometimes violent people, feuding and fighting. Some ventured farther west to the North American coast.

► Raids on Britain. Invasions of Vikings were difficult to stop. The Anglo-Saxon king Alfred halted them in 886 and reoccupied London. But a large area of Britain—known as the Danelaw—fell under Viking control. Not until the mid-10th century were they fully overcome.

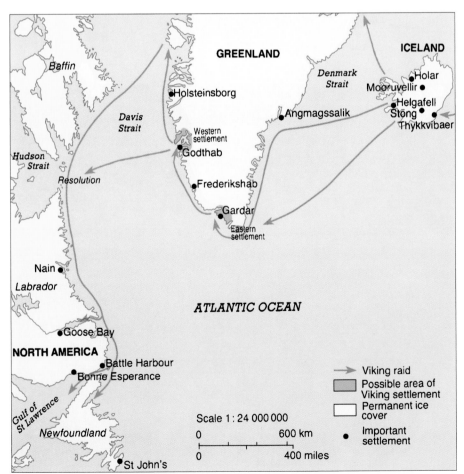

The Byzantine Empire

TODAY WE USE THE WORD BYZANTINE to describe the East Roman Empire and Byzantium for the city of Constantinople. Constantine the Great, the Christian emperor of Rome, made this ancient city (Byzantium) the capital of the East Roman Empire in 330. You have read earlier (page 16) how some parts of the West Roman Empire were lost to various barbarians, such as the Vandals, and how the Emperor Justinian later won back some territory.

The threat from the east

The greatest threat to the Byzantine Empire—the Holy Christian Empire—was from the Muslims in the east. Their religion was Islam, following their prophet Muhammad who lived in the seventh century, and they fought to establish their religion in other countries. By the eighth century they had occupied not only West Asia but also North Africa, Spain, and Portugal. The Byzantines held out against Islam, however. In the ninth century, under emperors from Macedonia in northern Greece, they began to push the Muslims back into Syria, and they later conquered the Bulgars in the north.

Constantinople

From the time of the first Macedonian emperors in 867, for about two centuries, Constantinople flourished. The Greek Orthodox Church began to send out missionaries to convert the unbelievers to Christianity. The empire grew. Its capital city, Constantinople, also grew within the walls built by the emperor Theodosius in the fifth century. The modern Turkish city there, called Istanbul, now fills the area laid out by Theodosius.

Constantinople was attacked many times in its history but the Byzantine Empire lasted until 1453, when the Ottoman Turks conquered the city.

Revival of the East Roman (Byzantine) Empire
May 11 330 Constantinople founded.
717–41 Reign of Emperor Leo III, who drives off Muslim attacks.
867 Beginning of reign of Basil I, first of the Macedonian emperors.
976–1025 Reign of Emperor Basil II, who conquers the Bulgars. Byzantine Empire at full extent by the end of his reign.
1176 Turkish Seljuks defeat the Byzantine emperor Manuel I.
May 23 1453 Ottoman Turks take Constantinople. Byzantine Empire collapses.

▼ The Byzantine Empire, showing its fullest extent by about 1025. The people known as the Bulgars were converted to the Orthodox Christian religion in 864, and their territory was conquered in 1018.

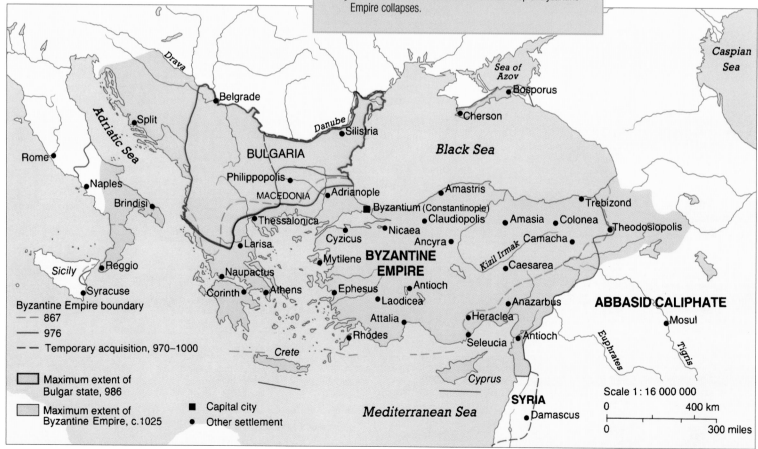

► The Roman emperor Justinian built the magnificent new church of Santa Sophia (it means Holy Wisdom) in Constantinople in 537. This is a view of it in 1852 by the architect Fossati, who was commissioned by the Turkish sultan to restore it. It had been converted to an Islamic mosque in 1453.

▲ This little drawing of Constantinople, made in 1436, shows the great domed roof of the church of Santa Sophia and a statue of the Emperor Justinian on a horse.

The Plantagenet Empire

THE EMPIRE OF CHARLEMAGNE HAD stretched across the countries we now know as France, Italy, and western Germany. His Empire was eventually divided into three parts for his grandsons in 843. By this time there were also other divisions of territory created by powerful lords —dukes and counts—who had small armies to control their own lands.

Saxon England

Since the Roman period England had been invaded and settled by different groups, first the Saxons, then the Danes. By the mid-11th century the king was Edward the Confessor, descended from Saxon and Norman families. On his death in 1066 there was no adult male in his family to succeed him. Harold Godwine, Earl of Wessex and the king's brother-in-law, claimed the throne.

Normandy and England

However, William, Duke of Normandy, had other ideas. He invaded England in 1066, winning the Battle of Hastings and the throne of England. From then the histories of France and England were linked together, and the English king played an important part in continental affairs. Over the next 140 years England and Normandy were usually ruled by one person, although at times the two countries were split between different kings.

The Plantagenet family

The Angevin family, whose base was at Anjou in France, are called Plantagenets by historians. The name Plantagenet may have come from the sprig of a plant (possibly a yellow broom plant) worn by Geoffrey of Anjou on his cap.

In December 1154 Henry II, the 21-year-old son of Matilda of England and Geoffrey of Anjou, came to England as king after the death of his cousin Stephen. Henry was already Duke of Normandy and of Aquitaine. He then led expeditions far into neighboring territories (building strong castles to impose his control) and increased the Plantagenet Empire. The lands he eventually controlled stretched from the borders of Scotland to the Pyrenees, but this empire was not to last.

▶ The Plantagenet Empire. The empire was bordered on the east by the lands of the king of France and on the south by various lordships. Henry II moved about his territory even when he was not fighting. He spent most of his time close to hunting reserves and frontiers—the Thames Valley, Southampton, Barfleur, and the Seine Valley.

◀ Henry II had a number of strong stone castles built, especially along coasts, which were open to attack. In England, Dover Castle was built by Henry II (although it has been added to over the years). So was Orford Castle in Suffolk, pictured here. Orford Castle took eight years to complete at a cost of more than £1,400—a fortune in the 12th century. The keep, the strongest part, and some earthworks still survive.

Boundary of Plantagenet Empire, 1154
Ruled by Stephen until 1154
Ruled by Henry II from 1149
Acquired by Henry II, 1151
Acquired by Henry II, 1152
Acquired by Henry II, 1154–1189
Disputed land
Boundary of Plantagenet Empire in France, 1226
Toulouse, 1154
▲ Castle
● Other settlement

Scale 1 : 5 000 000

0 ——— 150 km
0 ——— 100 miles

North Sea

ATLANTIC OCEAN

English Channel

Bay of Biscay

Mediterranean Sea

Plantagenet power

In France: Henry II becomes duke of Normandy in **1149**, count of Anjou in **1151**, and duke of Aquitaine in **1152**.

England in 1154: Stephen is king of England until his death in **1154** (duke of Normandy 1135–44). Henry II becomes king.

Campaigns:
1157, 1163, 1165 Wales.
1159 Toulouse. **1166** Britanny.

New territories acquired:
1159 Quercy.
1171 Britanny (by the marriage of Henry II's son, Geoffrey).
1174 Henry is recognized as lord in Ireland and in Scotland, but never rules there.

Ireland
Armagh ●
Granard ●
● Tuam
▲ Athlone
▲ Birr ● Dublin
Trimahoe ▲ ● ▲ Athy
Limerick ▲ ▲ Leighlin
● Cashel
Ardfinnan ▲
Lismore ▲ ● Waterford

Scotland
▲ Linlithgow
▲ Edinburgh ● Berwick
Kelso ●
▲ Ayr ● Roxburgh
Dumfries ▲
Carlisle ▲
Newcastle ▲
Richmond ▲
Lancaster ●
York ▲
Pontefract ▲
Conisborough ▲
Lincoln ●

Wales / England
Deganwy
Beaumaris ▲ Rhuddlan ▲
Caernarvon ▲ ● Chester
Conway ▲ Hawarden ▲
Shrewsbury ●
Leicester ●
Norwich ▲
Aberystwyth ▲
Builth ▲
Coventry ●
Cardigan ▲
Hereford ●
Orford ▲
Colchester ●
Pembroke ▲
Llandaff ●
Thames
London ▲
Canterbury ▲
Wells ●
Dover
Salisbury ●
Hastings ●
Southampton ●
Winchester ● Chichester ●
Exeter ●

France
Barfleur ●
Seine Rouen ●
▲ Château Gaillard
● Bayeux
Evreux ●
NORMANDY
St Pol de Léon ● St Malo ●
Avranches ●
● St Brieuc
MAINE
FRANCE
BRITTANY
Rennes ●
Le Mans ●
Vannes ●
Tours ●
Nantes ● *Loire*
ANJOU ▲ Chinon
Loudun ▲ **TOURAINE**
Mirbeau ▲ ● Bourges
POITOU
Poitiers ●
LA MARCHE
Clermont-Ferrand ●
● Saintes
AUVERGNE
AQUITAINE
VELAY
Périgueux ●
● Mende
Bordeaux ●
Cahors ●
Garonne
QUERCY Uzès ●
Agen ●
Albi ● Lodève ●
GASCONY
Aire ● **TOULOUSE**
Auch ● Toulouse ● Béziers ●
Bayonne ● ● Maguelone
Lescar ●
Oloron ● Comminges ● Narbonne ●
NAVARRE **FOIX**
PYRENEES **ARAGON**

The Bayeux Tapestry

THE FAMOUS BAYEUX TAPESTRY IS AN exciting account in pictures and in words of the events that led to the successful Norman invasion of England in 1066.

It begins: "EDWARD REX. UBI HAROLD DUX ANGLORUM ET SUI MILITES EQUITANT AD BOSHAM." This text, in Latin, provides the caption for the picture-story. It means "Edward the King. Where Harold, Duke of the English, and his soldiers ride to Bosham."

Harold and William

When King Edward of England died in 1066 there were two powerful leaders who claimed the throne— Harold, the English duke, and William, Duke of Normandy. At the beginning of the tapestry we learn that Harold traveled to Normandy and swore to support William. But as soon as Edward died, Harold claimed the English throne for himself. William prepared for invasion and war in England. He built a great fleet and on September 28 sailed to Pevensey in Sussex on the south coast of England. The Normans landed their army, horses, and supplies and then built a timber-and-earth castle at Hastings. Meanwhile Harold hurried south after defeating King Harald of Norway near York in northeast England.

▼ The Bayeux Tapestry is not a true tapestry because it was not woven. The pictures and words are embroidered in colored wools on linen. It is more than 230 ft (70 m) long. William's half-brother, Bishop Odo of Bayeux, probably ordered it to be made. The work was completed in England and then taken to France to be displayed at Bayeux Cathedral.

The battle of Hastings

William had an army of about 7,000, including 2,000 cavalrymen. The English army was smaller but fought well at a place that was later named Battle. The tapestry gives all the gory detail of the battle—arrows and spears fly through the air and men are cut down. Finally, Harold is wounded and killed. The English have a new Norman king—William the Conqueror.

Rediscovering the tapestry

Although the tapestry remained safe in the cathedral at Bayeux, it was not discovered to be an important historical "document" until the 18th century. It was moved several times during World War II, but it is now on display to the public in a special building.

◀ The tapestry is a rich source of illustrations of the 11th century. It shows a number of buildings, such as churches, castles, and towers. William's invasion fleet has ships built in the Viking style (longboats and clinker-built boats).

▼ The battle scenes show us how men fought at the time and the weapons and armor they carried: conical helmets with nose protectors, chain mail, shields, swords, and axes. Here King Harold is wounded with a Norman arrow and then cut down.

Domesday Book

T HERE ARE MANY DIFFERENT KINDS OF written evidence for the medieval period. They include histories, surveys, laws, court hearings, wills, and inventories (lists) of property in houses. Some of these documents have survived and can be studied today.

King William's survey

The Bayeux Tapestry provides evidence for William the Conqueror's invasion of England following his victory at the Battle of Hastings in 1066. Another important document has survived to help us understand what the conquered land of England was like—this time a written record.

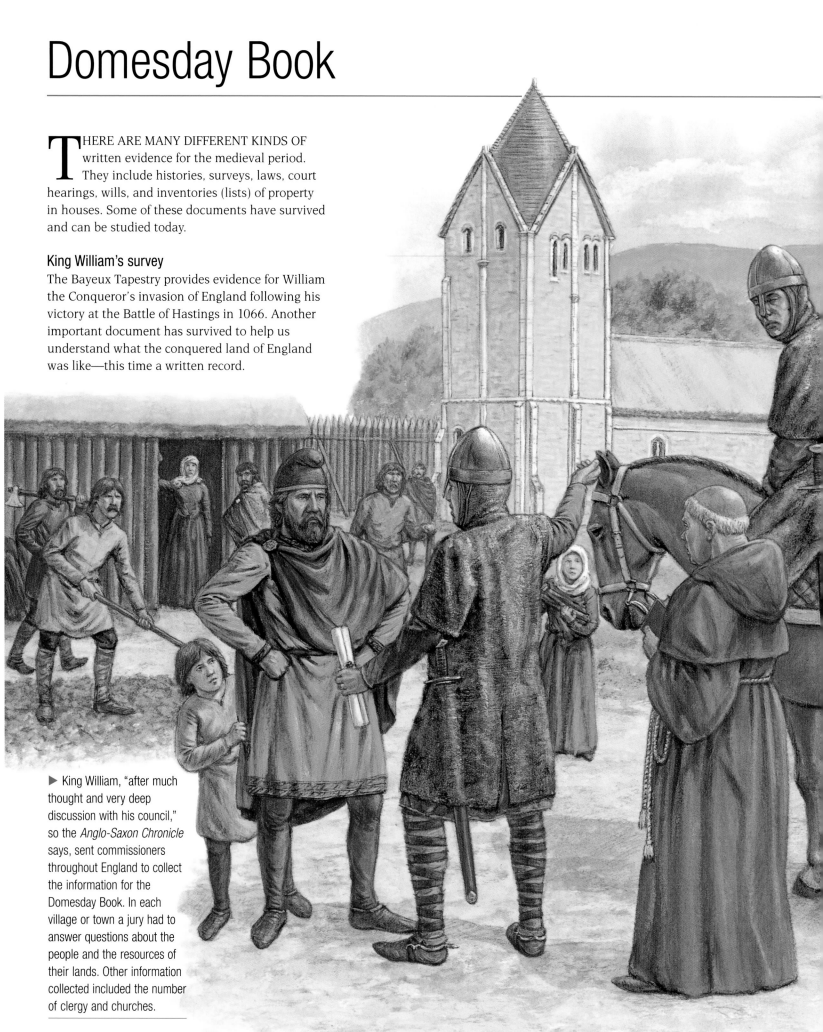

▶ King William, "after much thought and very deep discussion with his council," so the *Anglo-Saxon Chronicle* says, sent commissioners throughout England to collect the information for the Domesday Book. In each village or town a jury had to answer questions about the people and the resources of their lands. Other information collected included the number of clergy and churches.

In 1086 King William ordered a survey of all his English lands to check that he was receiving all the rents and taxes to which he was entitled. This survey came to be known as the Domesday Book and was referred to for many years afterward. In fact, there are two volumes of records. The Great Domesday surveys most of England, while the Little Domesday covers only the counties of Essex, Norfolk, and Suffolk. Not every place was recorded—the towns of Winchester and London and large parts of the north of England were left out. The Domesday volumes are kept today in the Public Record Office in London.

What is recorded?

King William wanted a record of who owned the land at the time of his invasion of England and who held the land 20 years later. The Domesday Book records this as "then" (before 1066) and "now" (in 1086). It states that William gave land to friends, such as Odo, the bishop of Bayeux, who fought with him at Hastings. It also records the number of plow teams a village had. Most of the population were "villeins" and "bordars," who were villagers who held varying amounts of land in the estate or village. "Slaves" were owned by the lord and had no land for themselves.

The Domesday Book also gives some information about animals and the amount of land available for feeding and pasturing animals. If the village had other resources, such as fishponds, mills, beehives, and saltworks, they too were recorded.

Translation of the Domesday Book entry (boxed area):

Brictmer, a thane of King Edward's, held FOBBING for 5 hides, as one manor. Now Count Eustace holds it in lordship.

Always 4 plows in lordship; 5 men's plows.

Then 8 villagers, now 3; then 8 smallholders, now 22; then 12 slaves, now 6.

Woodland, 700 pigs; pasture, 700 sheep; 1/2 fishery. 31 pigs, 717 sheep.

▲ The entry in the Domesday Book for the village of Fobbing in Essex tells us that Brictmer was lord of the manor under the Saxon king Edward the Confessor. King William gave Fobbing to Eustace, count of Boulogne, who fought at the Battle of Hastings. The entry shows that in 1066 there were eight villeins (tenants), in 1086 only three, and so on. The entry finishes with a list of other resources.

◀ An aerial photograph of Onley, Northamptonshire, a village in medieval times, now deserted except for a modern farm on the site. What you can see are the earthworks—the only remains of fields, gardens, houses, and streets. The most striking feature is the way the fields were plowed in strips, leaving furrows on each side.

Around the barn (top center) is the village with "hollow ways," or deeply cut tracks, running through it. On each side are individual plots of land for the villagers.

The Crusades

IN THE AREAS OF EUROPE THAT HAD BECOME Christian—Christendom is the general name often used—there were many devout followers of the religion. Religious "orders" were set up, and followers lived in religious communities of monks and nuns. Special religious objects (such as the bones of a saint) and holy places (shrines) were treated with great respect. From the fourth century, within the Roman Empire people made special journeys called pilgrimages to these holy places.

The Holy Land of Palestine was the most important destination for pilgrims. But the shrines of St. Peter and St. Paul in Rome became popular among pilgrims, especially after Jerusalem was taken by the Muslims in 638.

The Holy Land—lost to Christians

The Arab Muslims, followers of the prophet Muhammad, did not stop Christians from visiting the Holy Land. However, in 1076 Turkish Muslims captured Jerusalem from the Arabs. They turned Christians away, arresting and torturing some pilgrims. The Christian emperor in Constantinople called for help in fighting these Turks.

Fighting for Christ

To help the emperor, Pope Urban II in 1095 called for a "crusade" (war of the cross) to win back the Holy Land from the "unbelievers." Huge numbers joined

the cause and "took up the cross." The First Crusade won back Jerusalem within four years, killing the inhabitants and establishing a kingdom there.

Other crusades followed. There were many problems—not only in fighting the enemy but between the "Latin" Christians, who were led by Rome, and the "Greek," or "Orthodox," Christians whose capital was Constantinople.

▲ Krak des Chevaliers in Syria, a huge castle built by crusaders. Krak was held by the Knights of St. John the Hospitallers (an order of knights dedicated to defending the sick) from 1142 to 1271.

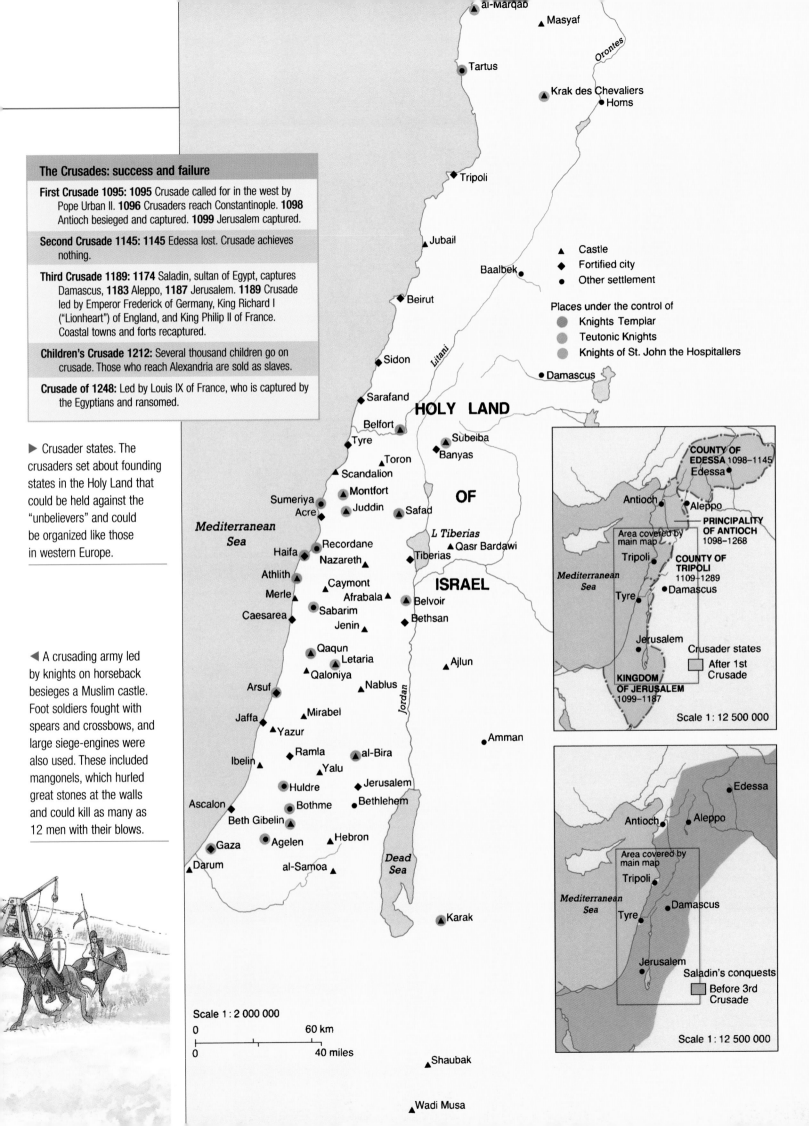

The Crusades: success and failure

First Crusade 1095: 1095 Crusade called for in the west by Pope Urban II. **1096** Crusaders reach Constantinople. **1098** Antioch besieged and captured. **1099** Jerusalem captured.

Second Crusade 1145: 1145 Edessa lost. Crusade achieves nothing.

Third Crusade 1189: 1174 Saladin, sultan of Egypt, captures Damascus, **1183** Aleppo, **1187** Jerusalem. **1189** Crusade led by Emperor Frederick of Germany, King Richard I ("Lionheart") of England, and King Philip II of France. Coastal towns and forts recaptured.

Children's Crusade 1212: Several thousand children go on crusade. Those who reach Alexandria are sold as slaves.

Crusade of 1248: Led by Louis IX of France, who is captured by the Egyptians and ransomed.

▶ Crusader states. The crusaders set about founding states in the Holy Land that could be held against the "unbelievers" and could be organized like those in western Europe.

◀ A crusading army led by knights on horseback besieges a Muslim castle. Foot soldiers fought with spears and crossbows, and large siege-engines were also used. These included mangonels, which hurled great stones at the walls and could kill as many as 12 men with their blows.

▲ Castle
◆ Fortified city
● Other settlement

Places under the control of
● Knights Templar
● Teutonic Knights
● Knights of St. John the Hospitallers

al-Marqab
Masyaf
Orontes
Tartus
Krak des Chevaliers
Homs
Tripoli
Jubail
Baalbek
Beirut
Litani
Sidon
Damascus
Sarafand
HOLY LAND
Belfort
Tyre
Subeiba
Banyas
Toron
OF
Scandalion
Montfort
Sumeriya
Juddin
Safad
Acre
Mediterranean Sea
L Tiberias
Recordane
Qasr Bardawi
Haifa
Nazareth
Tiberias
Athlith
ISRAEL
Caymont
Merle
Afrabala
Belvoir
Caesarea
Sabarim
Bethsan
Jenin
Qaqun
Letaria
Ajlun
Qaloniya
Nablus
Arsuf
Jordan
Mirabel
Jaffa
Yazur
Ramla
al-Bira
Ibelin
Yalu
Amman
Huldre
Jerusalem
Ascalon
Bothme
Bethlehem
Beth Gibelin
Gaza
Agelen
Hebron
Darum
al-Samoa
Dead Sea
Karak
Shaubak
Wadi Musa

Scale 1 : 2 000 000

0 ———— 60 km
0 ———— 40 miles

COUNTY OF EDESSA 1098–1145
Edessa
Antioch
Aleppo
Area covered by main map
PRINCIPALITY OF ANTIOCH 1098–1268
Tripoli
COUNTY OF TRIPOLI 1109–1289
Mediterranean Sea
Tyre
Damascus
Jerusalem
Crusader states
KINGDOM OF JERUSALEM 1099–1187
After 1st Crusade

Scale 1 : 12 500 000

Antioch
Edessa
Aleppo
Area covered by main map
Tripoli
Mediterranean Sea
Tyre
Damascus
Jerusalem
Saladin's conquests
Before 3rd Crusade

Scale 1 : 12 500 000

The German Empire

THE WEST ROMAN EMPIRE HAD A LONG and complicated history. Previous maps show how it emerged from earlier empires to become the most important state in Europe. From 962 it was called the Holy Roman Empire. Earlier in this period it is sometimes called the Saxon Empire, because it was ruled by Saxon kings. The rulers of the Empire were all Germans.

King Henry of Germany

The lands of Germany were divided into duchies, lands belonging to dukes. Each duke was powerful and had his own army and castles. They recognized kings but often fought against them. In 919 Henry, Duke of Saxony, succeeded the previous king, Conrad of Franconia. At first Henry had authority over only these two areas, but he was eventually recognized as Henry I throughout Germany.

Enemies on the borders

The Germans had two main enemies: the Magyars (Hungarians) and the Slavs. Henry I tricked the Magyars into a truce while he built castles and fortress towns, such as Quedlinburg and Merseburg. In the war of 933 he defeated them. The Slavs were more difficult because they had settled in large numbers and were farming lands north of the Elbe River. Gradually, however, the German kings extended their territory eastward.

Otto I—emperor

Henry's son Otto came to the throne in 936. He made the German dukes his subjects. One writer at the time said that the dukes "gave him their lands and promised him their loyalty and help against all enemies." Otto (sometimes known as Otto the Great) attacked the Magyars and finally defeated them in 955. He extended his authority in other ways, too. In 951 he became king of Italy and he was crowned Holy Roman Emperor in 962.

The Holy Roman Empire

Otto saw himself as the natural successor to the emperor Charlemagne. His title was Imperator Augustus—Emperor Augustus. To maintain his authority, Otto installed his own cousin as pope—Gregory VI—in 996. In 998 his grandson Otto III proclaimed that the old Roman Empire was now revived. The people of Rome itself, however, never really liked these German emperors and rose up against Otto, forcing him to flee the city.

◄ Scenes from the life of Pope Gregory VII (1073–85), from the bishop of Freising's *World Chronicle*. Emperor Henry IV of Germany campaigned in Italy against the Pope. These four scenes describe the dispute, and show more sympathy for Gregory (top center and right) than for Henry (top left). They also give an early example of how history could be tellingly depicted by pictures from this period.

▲ The German Empire (Holy Roman Empire). The main boundaries show how the Empire grew. The kingdoms of Italy and Burgundy were absorbed into the Empire in the 10th and 11th centuries, but the Lombards of northern Italy were always troublesome. Noble families and princes became increasingly powerful in Germany itself. A march was a frontier territory that was often disputed with the neighboring kingdom or country. It was heavily militarized at all times. A duchy was a territory that was controlled by a duke (or duchess) and that had its own laws. Associated states were, at various times, ruled by their own kings.

◄ A drawing from a manuscript of 1425 shows a panmaker at work in Nuremburg, Germany. The panmaker is using a pointed hammer to pierce the bowl-shaped metal utensil repeatedly to produce a colander for straining. A medieval kitchen would have contained many of the cooking utensils we know today.

German expansion

919–36	Henry I is king of Germany. Campaigns against the Slavs and Magyars.
955	Otto I finally defeats the Magyars.
967–70	Attempts to gain territory in southern Italy.
1033	Kingdom of Burgundy added to empire.
1158	Kingdom of Bohemia added to empire.
1158	March of Lausitz, **1163** Duchy of Silesia, Opol, and Ratibor, and **1181** Duchy of Pomerania under German control.
1194	Kingdom of Sicily acquired by Henry VI.
1231	Teutonic Knights win Prussia.

The Medieval Church

THE CHRISTIAN CHURCH DEVELOPED slowly at first in the Roman world. By the third century Christianity was spreading quickly. Bishops were in charge of Christian worship in communities all over the Roman Empire.

Being a Christian was not always easy in the Roman world, but after 312 Christians were not persecuted for their religion. Christianity finally became the "official" religion of the Roman Empire in 395 under the emperor Theodosius.

Christian monks

The word "monk" comes from the Greek word for alone—*monos*. The first Christian monks lived alone, away from other communities, in the Egyptian desert. The first religious communities of nuns were also established in Egypt. Monks and nuns did not marry and they lived separate from society, without any comforts or luxuries.

The idea of the monastic life spread through the Roman world, not only in the eastern Mediterranean but also in North Africa, Italy, Gaul (France), Britain, and beyond the Roman provinces in Ireland.

Medieval monasteries

After the Roman period many monasteries were founded that followed the Rule (or code) of St. Benedict. Other "orders" of monks and nuns were also established. For example, a community was established in 909 at Cluny in Burgundy. By the next century there were 1,450 Cluniac communities throughout western Europe. Monasteries were important places of pilgrimage and learning.

The organization of Christianity

The system of organizing Christianity for the community was set up in the Roman period. Bishops were appointed to areas called dioceses. Priests or vicars served individual communities in parishes within dioceses. A church was built for each community, but its size and structure depended on what each parish could afford.

The shape and architecture of the parish church varied enormously across the Christian world. In theory, all Western religious communities looked to Rome and the pope as the central authority. Often, though, communities acted as they thought best.

▲ An illustrated letter B from a bible now in Winchester, England. The bible was originally made for the bishop of Winchester, Henry of Blois, in the late 12th century. Part of the picture shows Jesus driving out devils.

▶ This illustration from the 12th century shows a monk making a copy of the Bible. These beautifully illustrated handmade books were highly treasured, but only a few survive today from the early periods.

▲ ▶ The church at Wroxeter in Shropshire, England, stands in one corner of a Roman town, most of which is now hidden under grass fields. There may have been a Christian community here in the Roman period. In the ninth century a decorated Anglo-Saxon cross must have stood in the churchyard (above). Parts of this cross survive in the wall of the aisle of the church.

Most parish churches in Britain have a long history (right). There may have been a church here before the one built in the seventh or eighth century. The Anglo-Saxon builders used large stones from the Roman town to construct their nave and chancel. The Domesday Book (pages 32–33) records four priests here in 1086.

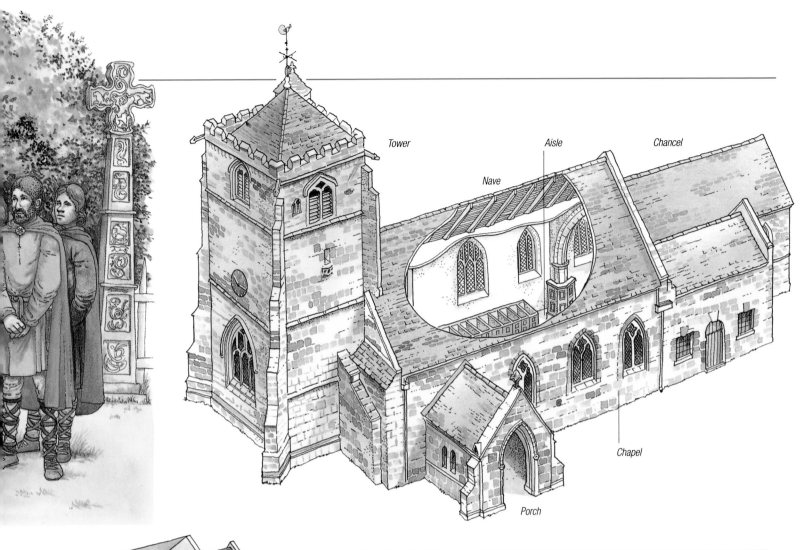

Tower

Nave

Aisle

Chancel

Chapel

Porch

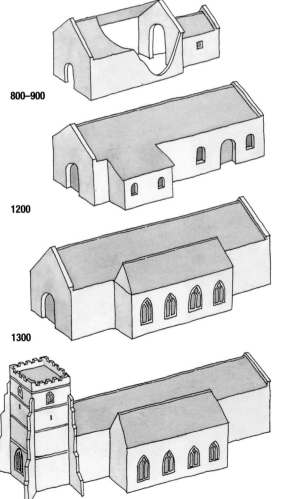

800–900

1200

1300

1400

▲ ▶ The church at Wroxeter today has additions from many centuries. The entrance is through the 19th-century porch. In the medieval period porches were often used to conduct parish business.

The aisle allowed more people to stand in the congregation at services, and there was often a chapel in the aisle (as here), built by a wealthy person as a place for the priest to pray for the soul.

The nave was where the congregation stood (there were usually no seats in a medieval church). The priest conducted the service in the chancel. The tower had the bells to summon the people to the service.

This view of Wroxeter Church (right) shows the Anglo-Saxon nave and the tower, which was built later.

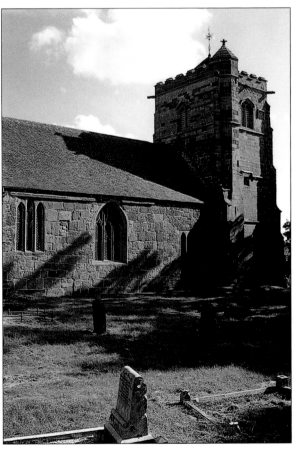

Education

IN THE MEDIEVAL PERIOD, FOR MOST PEOPLE education or learning, either reading or writing, served no practical purpose. There were many people—both workers and the wealthy—who could not read or write. But the clergy in the churches did need to be educated.

Literature from earlier periods

Manuscripts from the Romans (and a few Greek ones) survived long enough for monks to copy them out and to study them. Not all those involved in religion were educated, however. But clergy who served country parishes needed skills in reading, writing, and music, since few children were able to attend schools.

Schools

Schools were established for children, either as part of monasteries or by the bishop. For example, Lanfranc, who was appointed archbishop of Canterbury, England, in 1070, set up a school at Canterbury for local children.

Parish priests also did some teaching. The 12th-century historian Ordericus Vitalis was sent to a priest in Shrewsbury, England, at the age of five

◀ Nicholas of Lyra, seen teaching here in the center, was a monk from Normandy who taught at the University of Paris in the 14th century. Like most other teachers, he gave lectures to his students in a very formal way.

and learned reading, grammar, and music before taking holy orders to become a monk.

Universities

Places where students could continue their studies for longer were being established by the church from the 12th century onward, in particular for priests and monks to attend. The most famous universities were established in Paris (for philosophy and religion), Bologna in northern Italy (for law), and Salerno in southern Italy (for medicine). In England the first colleges were founded in Oxford and Cambridge in the 13th century.

▶ Hugh of St. Victor teaching in his monastery at St. Victor in Paris. Hugh became the prior, or leader, of the college in 1133. This was a college of canons who followed the Rule of St. Augustine. A canon was a clerk who lived according to a Rule (the word in Greek for "rule" is *kanon*). The illustration here is from one of Hugh's own works in a manuscript edition made in the 13th century. This copy is now in the Bodleian Library of Oxford University, England.

◀ The medieval university of Bologna, northern Italy, was grouped in two areas, close to each other, inside the walls of the city. The famous law school was in the center. The building you can see here, in the center of the medieval university area, is the Palazzo of King Enzo, built in 1246 and used as his prison for 23 years until his death in 1272. The university grew very quickly during these years.

Cathedral-building

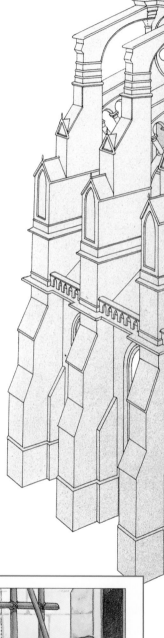

E KNOW THAT CATHEDRALS ARE usually large, grand churches, but the word itself can be traced back to the Romans. In Latin *cathedra* means professor's, or teacher's, chair. The word was used in the medieval period in exactly the same way—both Hugh and Nicholas are illustrated seated at their cathedra on pages 40–41. The word "seat" came to mean "important church," because a cathedral was where the seat or throne of the bishop of the diocese was.

Size and shape

Cathedrals are usually large buildings, but it is possible to find some ordinary parish churches in England, for example, which are even larger than cathedrals. A cathedral was also either secular (meaning that it was served by canons who were clerks) or monastic (served by monks).

A secular cathedral building would stand on its own like a big church. A monastic cathedral would be a church building attached to a whole group of other buildings in which the monks lived and worked. There would be, for example, a chapter house (for daily meetings, announcements, and sometimes punishments), a refectory (dining room), an infirmary (hospital), kitchens, a dormitory (large room for sleeping), a lavatorium (for washing), and a reredorter (lavatory).

A new style of building

In the middle of the 12th century in France a completely new style of church-building was developed. The Gothic style with its elaborate architecture and glass-filled windows allowed the

building dedicated to God to be filled with "the new light," as one writer put it.

These buildings were very expensive and often took many years to complete. Gervase, a monk at the cathedral church at Canterbury, southern England, wrote in 1174:

"The master-mason, William of Sens, began to prepare all that was necessary for the new building and to destroy what was there before. This took the first year. In the next year he put up four pillars and after the winter two more . . ."

A master-mason might work with about 30 experienced craftsmen who traveled from job to job. Masons (stonecutters) cut their own special mark in each stone they carved so that they could be paid for this "piecework." Local people would be brought in for the unskilled jobs, such as carrying stone.

Columns, aisles, and arches

This new style of architecture involved new types of building techniques, which the planners and stonemasons had to invent and then test. The techniques did not always work—occasionally buildings even fell down.

Cathedrals needed to hold large congregations of people, but they also had to look as if they were worthy to be called "houses for God." The builders of Gothic architecture were the first people to discover how to put up very tall buildings of stone without enormously thick walls to carry all that weight, using flying buttresses as a means of support. This discovery allowed them to design and build churches that looked beautiful both inside and out.

▼ Cathedral-building involved lifting enormous blocks of stone. Two types of crane are shown here—the winch (left) and the treadwheel (right).

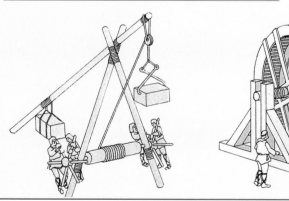

▶ Masons needed great skill in order to cut and carve stone accurately.

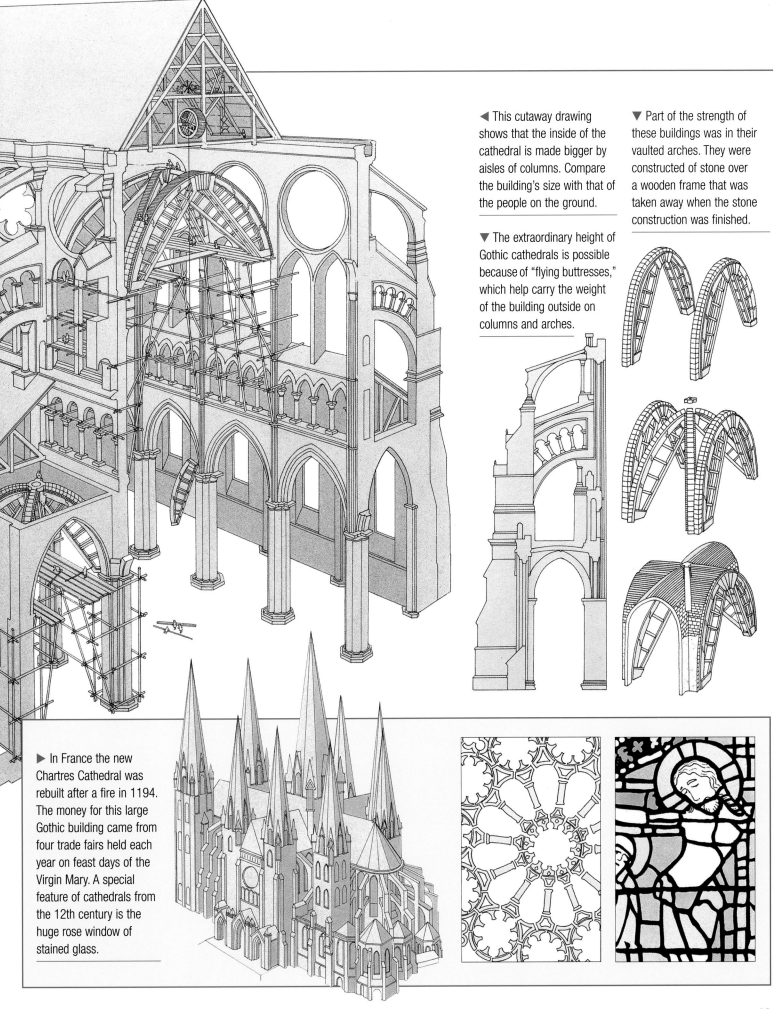

◀ This cutaway drawing shows that the inside of the cathedral is made bigger by aisles of columns. Compare the building's size with that of the people on the ground.

▼ The extraordinary height of Gothic cathedrals is possible because of "flying buttresses," which help carry the weight of the building outside on columns and arches.

▼ Part of the strength of these buildings was in their vaulted arches. They were constructed of stone over a wooden frame that was taken away when the stone construction was finished.

▶ In France the new Chartres Cathedral was rebuilt after a fire in 1194. The money for this large Gothic building came from four trade fairs held each year on feast days of the Virgin Mary. A special feature of cathedrals from the 12th century is the huge rose window of stained glass.

Stories in Stained Glass

"The church shines, with its middle part brightened."

THE "NEW LIGHT" DESCRIBED BY ABBOT Suger, the leader of a community of monks in the early 12th century, was brought about in churches and cathedrals by the lightness of the building, towering to the sky, and by the light that streamed in through the windows. Not just white light came in—the light was made all the colors of the rainbow by stained glass.

Creating an atmosphere

Churches and cathedrals were built to honor God. Those responsible for the building may have wanted to show how wealthy and powerful they were, but it was even more important to create the right atmosphere for those who came to worship. Gothic churches, as we have seen, were therefore very impressive buildings—it is almost impossible not to wonder at them.

The atmosphere inside the church was created by sculpture, paintings, and the elaborate ceremonies full of chanting and music. Perhaps even more important was the "feel" created by the stained glass all around. Like the glittering effect of Byzantine mosaics, stained glass helped the worshipers feel they really were in a special place.

Stories in the window

Many people could not read so they were unable to discover for themselves the stories in the Bible or to learn from them, as their priests wanted them to. Stained glass and also wall paintings allowed them to "read" the stories for themselves.

In many cases, however, it would be difficult to get more than just an impression of the story, because the windows in cathedrals were so high up. The story of Christ's life, and especially his death, was a favorite subject. The saints (there were a great number of them in the medieval world) and their lives were often pictured, too.

Making a window

It is easy to appreciate from the pictures shown here that making stained-glass windows was a skilled job. Glass was made from a mixture of ash from the wood of beech trees and washed sand, heated to a very high temperature. The color produced was greenish and it was difficult to see through. To produce bright colors, different kinds of metal, such as iron and copper oxides, were added to the mixture.

The glass was then cut into pieces and joined together with strips of lead to make up the picture. The glass was also painted to produce the picture. Sections were held together with iron rods and fitted into the stone window frames.

Glass painters, like stonemasons, traveled from place to place to find work which they were commissioned to complete.

Chartres

One of the best buildings in which to see stained glass is Chartres Cathedral in northern France. After a disastrous fire in 1194, the cathedral was destroyed. It was rebuilt over a period of 26 years. Most of the medieval windows which were constructed and painted by craftspeople still survive today.

▶ A 13th-century window at Chartres Cathedral. Between 1200 and 1235 more than 100 stained-glass windows were made. This work was paid for by a variety of people, from King Louis IX to the count of Brittany and from the rich merchants in the city to the masons who worked on the building.

The scenes here are from Christ's last days—for example, the Last Supper and washing the feet of his disciples (bottom).

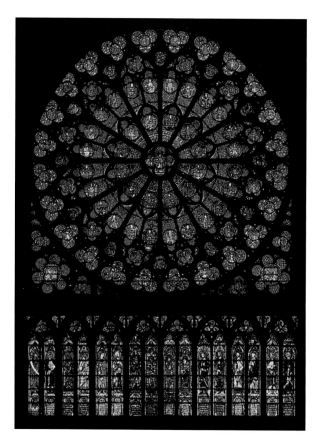

▲ This rose window is in the church of Notre Dame (Our Lady) in Paris. It was made by two craftsmen in about 1270. The shape of the window and the colors used allow light to sparkle through into the church.

▶ A chapel window in Strasbourg Cathedral, France, made in the mid-14th century. Later windows, such as this one, were made by painting on larger sheets of glass. The scenes here show the Resurrection of Christ.

Medieval Arts and Crafts

ONE OF THE MOST EXTRAORDINARY aspects of the medieval period in Europe is the range of works of art created by skilled craftspeople. Decoration was everywhere, from the complicated fronts of cathedrals to the metal clasps on bibles. All sorts of techniques were used, such as carving in stone and wood, metalwork, painting, stained glass, and tapestry making.

Builders in stone ...

You have seen before how stonemasons were used to create cathedrals to be wondered at. Sculptors provided decoration for both the inside and outside of these buildings—on windows, columns, and towers. Doorways especially were often highly decorated with intricate carvings of birds, horses, and leaves. Medieval cathedrals also had a great number of carvings of individual people in niches (indentations in walls), especially of people from the Bible, saints, popes, and kings.

... and in wood

Wood does not survive as well as stone, but there are still a great many examples of the medieval woodworker's craft. Wood was very important in building, especially up to the 12th century. Even after that most ordinary buildings were of wood. Skills were developed to create complex constructions in wood. A manuscript describes the new wooden tower of Ely Cathedral, England, in 1328 as:

"the ingenious wooden structure, designed with great and astonishing subtlety ... huge beams cut and cunningly made into frames for the work by clever craftsmen."

Writers

We have already seen some examples of literature from the medieval period. Historians have left us information about people and events in the past. There were also many poems and stories. The clergy wrote mainly in Latin, but gradually the languages that people spoke were used for literature too.

Stories that retold tales from the classical (Greek and Roman) periods were very popular. So was heroic poetry, usually recited aloud, praising the skills and exploits of warriors. There follows a short translated extract from *Beowulf*, a poem written in Old English in the eighth century about a Germanic hero who overcomes monsters but is finally slain by a dragon:

◀ Early surviving examples of wood carving, such as this small figure of the Virgin Mary from the church at Griske, Sunnøre, Norway, show that craftsmen of the period had already acquired great expressive power.

▶ A pattern book made in about 1380 showing various birds (the bullfinch is labeled). Pattern books were used by designers, wood carvers, and people doing embroidery.

▼ The wooden roof of a parish church in Garway, Herefordshire, England, shows the skill of local carpenters. The roof frames have beams that tie the outside walls together (tie beams), collar beams to hold the frame together, and braces.

Music

Music was very important in medieval life. A special way of singing psalms in monasteries was developed. It was known as chanting, and it became part of the monks' daily services. Plainchants (in unison) were sung in monasteries from the earliest periods. After the 11th century other lines of melody were added, and the chants became more complex.

Outside of religious life, traveling performers known as troubadours recited poetry and tales, and sang accompanied by instruments such as trumpets, bagpipes, and lutes. Troubadours entertained crowds at fairs, weddings, and other medieval celebrations.

▼ Pope Gregory the Great at his writing desk with his symbol, the dove. He was pope in the sixth century. This beautiful 10th-century carving is made of ivory (animal tusk) and was the cover of a book that is now kept in a museum in Vienna, Austria.

▼ This illustration from a medieval Spanish manuscript shows two musicians. The manuscript also has some lines of music drawn out (not shown here) to help singers accompany the players.

47

Science, Medicine, and Printing

THE MODERN WORD "SCIENCE" COMES from the Latin word *scientia*, meaning "a knowledge of." Classical and medieval people wanted a knowledge of a great many things that they saw around them but did not always understand. Knowledge and inventions from the Greeks and Romans passed to the East Roman Empire in Constantinople.

Muslim technology

Muslims in the east acquired this knowledge and developed it, collecting as much information as they could. For example, an 11th-century author, al-Bakri, says that the caliph (ruler) ordered a full survey to be made of the Roman aqueducts (which were built to provide Roman cities with a regular water supply) in northern Tunisia, so that ideas could be gained to develop their own system. The Muslims were skillful observers and recorders, and they invented accurate measuring instruments.

Passing on the knowledge

The Christian medieval world often came into contact with Muslims and their knowledge in the 12th century, particularly in Spain and Sicily. Scholars from Christian countries in Europe began to go to these countries to learn from, and to translate, the manuscripts they found there.

A number of inventions were very practical, such as the magnetic needle in the compass for navigation, or spectacles to discover the science of light. Many ideas were outlined. Some, such as the helicopter drawn by Leonardo da Vinci as early as 1486, were ahead of their time,

Medicine

The science of medicine and healing was well advanced in classical times. In the medieval period, though, herbs were the main source of treatment. Some remedies that doctors used then we do not use today. For example, the medieval treatment of bleeding with a leech (a blood-sucking water worm) probably prevented many people from getting better.

Medieval people believed in God's direct power over their bodies. The bubonic plague (the "Black Death"), which killed many thousands of people, was thought to be punishment from God. People's belief in the "influence" of the atmosphere around them to cause sickness gives us the name influenza. Folklore, the beliefs passed from generation to generation, played a major part in medicine and healing.

◄ Model of a gear and barrel-like spring system invented by Leonardo da Vinci (1452–1519), the Italian painter, sculptor, architect, engineer, and scientist.

▶ Page from a book on medicine written by a doctor in Baghdad in the 11th century. The text explains how squash can quench thirst and clean out the bowels.

▼ Astrolabes are for observing the sun and the moon and making accurate measurements. The astrolabe shown here was made by a Muslim in Spain in 1068.

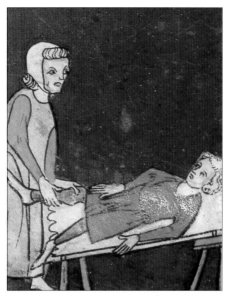

▲ Two of the 96 illustrations that were included in a textbook for doctors written by Roger of Salerno (in Italy) in about 1170. Here a doctor, dressed in the long gown of his profession, examines patients suffering from ailments in the leg and knee.

How printing developed

Passing on knowledge was difficult in the medieval world. There were schools and universities and there were books as well, but they had to be laboriously copied out by hand. There was no quick and easy way of reproducing ideas and information.

By the 14th century paper had not only been invented but was in good supply. Religious pictures, some with lettering added, could be produced by means of wood blocks (using the same method as a linocut or potato print today). Engraving was also used for illustrating books. Maps were printed from engravings in several German towns and in Venice.

The first printed book

The next stage was to make individual letters of metal that could be put together to make up a page of text. Printing from cast-metal type probably began in Korea in the 1390s, but in Europe it is first thought to have been developed by Johann Gutenberg in the town of Mainz in Germany. One of the earliest printed books using movable metal type was probably Gutenberg's *Book of Psalms* of 1457.

The idea was spread quickly by German printers to Paris, Venice, and Rome, and by 1500 there were 250 towns in Europe that had their own printing presses. Venice was an important center, with 150 presses at work there. Knowledge and new ideas soon spread throughout Europe in the form of books printed in a variety of languages.

▲ A printing press in about 1520. The press pushes the inked block onto individual sheets of paper.

▶ Two playing cards printed in about 1470. Printing was not used exclusively for serious purposes.

Part Two

The Lands of Medieval Europe

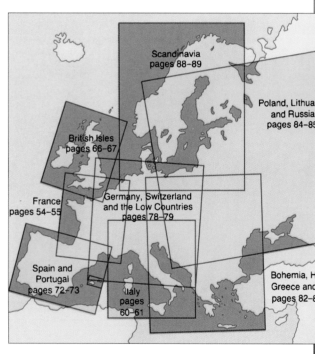

▲ Key to maps in this section of the book.

▶ A 14th-century illustration depicting a scene from *Roman de la Rose* (Romance of the Rose), a medieval love poem by two French writers, de Lorris and de Meung.

Travel

"Whan that Aprill with his shoures soote/
The droghte of Marche hath perced to the
roote . . . Thanne longen folk to goon
pilgrimages."

*"When in April the sweet showers fall and pierce the
drought of March to the root . . . then people long
to go on pilgrimages."*

THIS IS THE OPENING OF A LONG POEM
called *The Canterbury Tales* by Geoffrey Chaucer
written in the late 14th century. The poem is
about a group of people who join together to make
the five-day journey from London to Canterbury to
worship at the shrine of the murdered archbishop
St. Thomas à Becket.

During the medieval period all sorts of people
made long journeys, although travel was not nearly
as easy as it is today or even as it was in the Roman
period. Traveling musicians and actors entertained
pilgrims and others on the road and in the inns.

Roads

During the hundreds of years of the Roman Empire
a huge network of roads had been developed. It
allowed the army to move swiftly from one trouble
spot to another. It also allowed merchants to trade
across countries, and news and ideas to spread.

You can still see Roman roads in European
countries today, and they were certainly used by
people in the medieval period. There was no imperial
highway authority to maintain the roads (as there is
today), although local sections and bridges were
looked after and improved. Tolls (travel taxes) were
paid on some roads.

The Canterbury pilgrims did not choose to travel
very far, but many pilgrims did. They undertook
dangerous journeys right across Europe to Rome and
on to the Holy Land, or to the shrine of St. James the
Great in Compostela in northern Spain.

Staying the night

Travel in medieval times was not easy, comfortable,
or safe. There were few places where travelers could
put up for the night. Monasteries had a duty to
accommodate travelers, and if you were rich enough
you could stay at manor houses or castles on the
way. Others had to make do at inns, which were not
obviously dangerous. Most people traveled on
horseback, although an elaborate cart, called a char,
with a canvas roof was available in Chaucer's time.

▲ The Bayeux Tapestry
shows one of the ships built
for William the Conqueror's
invasion army of 1066. In
shape it is similar to Viking
boats. It has no oars but is
driven by sail, with a steering
rudder at the stern (back).

▼ Travelers in the early 16th
century in Holland arrive for
May Day celebrations on
horseback, on foot, and by
boat. The river boat is
paddled easily by one person.
The man on the prow fends
off the arches of the bridge.

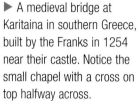

▶ A medieval bridge at
Karitaina in southern Greece,
built by the Franks in 1254
near their castle. Notice the
small chapel with a cross on
top halfway across.

▼ This 15th-century
illustration from *The Book of
Marvels* shows travelers from
Europe outside the walls of
Beijing (China). The artist did
not know what it looked like
and had to make up the view.

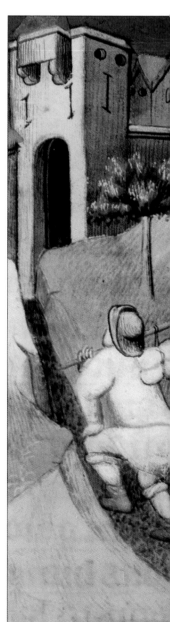

Moving goods

Merchants often traveled a great deal in order to find new commodities to sell. They also had to move their goods over long distances. Where possible, water transportation was used, as it had been since prehistoric times. It was cheaper and easier than road transport. Crusaders saw very different types of ships in the Mediterranean from those used in northern Europe.

Finding the way was much improved by medieval inventions, notably the compass and the astrolabe, The astrolabe was still used until the 18th century. New maps, as we shall see on pages 74–75, were in use from the 14th and 15th centuries onward.

France

MOST IMPORTANT CHANGES IN THE government of France took place in the 13th century under King Louis IX. He became king in 1226 and reigned until his death in 1270. If you look again at the map of the Plantagenet Empire (page 29) you will see the differences which had occurred. The map here shows the later situation in France and Belgium in the 13th century. The dukes of Burgundy ruled the large territory that included the land still known as Burgundy today, although it never became a state.

The reign of Louis IX (St. Louis)

Under previous kings of France the lands ruled directly by the king had been extended. But under Louis IX the kingdom did not grow. He wanted to put a stop to the violent way disputes were being settled and encourage people to use the law courts. The *parlement* was the main royal court of law. Some of the new territories were ruled by Louis' brothers; others were under the control of the king of England. For six years Louis fought a crusade against the Muslims. He was once captured and a ransom had to be paid before he was released.

At home, during his reign, he encouraged the development of education and the church. The first French universities were founded. In Paris there were many artists, masons, and sculptors employed on new works. Paris became the most important center of book production of the time.

◀ This illustration from a 15th-century French manuscript shows the assassination of John the Fearless, Duke of Burgundy, in 1419 at Montereau.

▲ Before the invention of machines, farmers used flails to beat the seed from cornstalks. Here a 15th-century French book shows this happening at harvesttime.

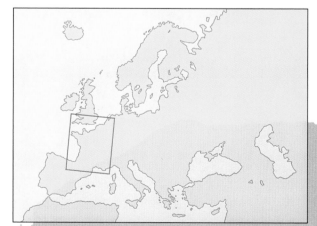

Important settlement

Features located at a settlement
Monastery
Castle
University

Boundary, 13th century

Feet
6,500
4,875
1,300
650
0

English Channel

Bruges
Ghent
St Omer
Tournai
Arras
Schelde
Somme
Arques
Corbie
Fécamp
Premontré
Rouen
Beauvais
Rethel
Château Gaillard
St Clair
Pierrefonds
Aisne
Caen
Seine
Reims
Coutances
Royaumont
Marne
Châlons
St Evroult
Paris
Mt St Michel
Montfort
Seine
St Pol de Léon
Sées
Etampes
Troyes
St Brieuc
Chartres
Les Clairets
Clairvaux
Rennes
Sens
Quimper
Le Mans
Orléans
Fleury
Pontigny
Langres
Montereau
Vannes
Vilaine
Flavigny
Beaulieu
Vézelay
Dijon
Loire
Angers
Tours
Amboise
Loire
Cher
Vézelay
Citeaux
Nantes
Fontevrault
Chinon
Loches
Autun
Thouars
FRANCE
Bourges
Nevers
La Ferté
Poitiers
Cluny
St Maixent
Saône
La Rochelle
Charroux
Charlieu
Vienne
Limoges
Saintes
Clermont-Ferrand
Angoulême
Ventadour
MASSIF
Périgueux
Brive-la-Gaillarde
Allier
Aurillac
CENTRAL
Le Puy
Bordeaux
Dordogne
Villandraut
Castillon
Cahors
Lot
Mende
Bazas
Garonne
Agen
Rodez
Moissac
Uzès
Tarn
Albi
Dax
La Couvertoirade
Lodève
Nîmes
Bayonne
Auch
Toulouse
Montpellier
Lescar
Montaner
Carcassonne
Aude
Narbonne
Lourdes
St Betrand
PYRENEES

Scale 1 : 4 000 000
0   100 km
0   80 miles

Mediterranean Sea

A   B   C   D

► The small village of La Couvertoirade in southern France was on one of the routes pilgrims took on their journey to the shrine of St. James the Great at Compostela in northern Spain. This village, built on a rock, was taken by the Templar Knights in 1182. The knights built a castle there in the early 13th century. The Order of Templars was set up to protect pilgrims to the Holy Lands. When the order was dissolved in 1312, La Couvertoirade passed to another order of knights, the Hospitallers, who defended the sick. The wall and towers you can see today were built in 1439. It is a fine example of a heavily fortified village.

▼ An illustration from a French book about hunting, *The Book of the Hunt*, written in the late 14th century by Gaston Fébus, Count of Foix. Here the hunters, in the middle of whom sits the count himself, prepare for a boar hunt.

Medieval Paris

THE MODERN CAPITAL CITY OF PARIS, France, takes its name from the Parisi tribe who lived in the area before the Romans invaded Gaul and founded a fishing village there. The earliest occupation was on the largest of the islands in the Seine River that now flows through the city.

The medieval capital

From the sixth century onward, Paris gradually developed beyond the Roman walls and suburbs. Swamps around the Seine River were drained, monasteries were built, and the town became wealthy. The king of the Franks, Clovis, made Paris his capital in 508, and when Hugh Capet, Count of Paris, became king of France in 987, Paris became the permanent capital. The Cathedral of Notre Dame (Our Lady) was completed in the 14th century.

Much of medieval Paris was destroyed during the reign of Louis XIV in the 17th century and later when Napoleon III (Louis Napoleon) built 60 new streets through the old town. These new wide streets were called boulevards.

▶ Medieval Paris. The twin towers of the Cathedral of Notre Dame dominate this view of the Île de la Cité, the island in the middle of the Seine River connected to the rest of the city by bridges. Barges brought goods to wharfs around the island, and houses and shops lined the wooden bridges.

▼ Paris during the 14th century. Nobles are attended by their servants in an illustration from Jean Froissart's accounts of life and war at the time. The city, crowded with houses and churches, is well protected by its wall, gates, and towers.

Paris

Italy

UNTIL THE MIDDLE OF THE SIXTH CENTURY Italy was still considered part of the Roman Empire. Then, in 568, it was invaded by the Lombards (a Germanic tribe that originated in southern Sweden). It was unique in medieval Europe because the king of the Lombards was always a foreigner and after 774 had no authority over the whole of what we know as Italy today. In the 10th century it was under the control of the German rulers. Some of the cities—such as Venice, Milan, and Florence—remained independent.

Five major powers

The powerful kings of Aragon, based in Catalonia in northeast Spain, gradually acquired more and more territory to include the Balearic Islands and then the islands farther east. In the 15th century they also took over the Kingdom of Naples.

By the early 15th century there were five major powers in Italy. The north was divided between the Duchy of Milan and the Venetian Republic. To the south, the Republic of Florence was the strongest state in Tuscany. In the center lay the Papal State (of Rome, ruled by the pope) and farther south was the Kingdom of Naples.

Powerful families and republics

In many territories power was held by committees of people elected to office—republics. This gradually changed as one powerful man or family emerged. For example, the Visconti family held Milan; the Medici family took over the Republic of Florence; and Venice was ruled by a head of state, a doge, who was elected for life.

Condottieri (mercenaries)

Towns, republics, duchies, and kingdoms were often at war. Local troops, called militia, protected most towns until the 14th century. A change then took place as towns began to buy the services of mercenary soldiers, called *condottieri*. They were often difficult to get rid of after the war, and towns were forced to continue paying for them—in effect, a sort of blackmail.

One such mercenary was Bartolomeo Colleoni, captain-general of the army of Venice. Colleoni died a very rich man in 1476.

▼ This map of Rome was made in 1323 by Paolo di Venezia. It shows some of the monuments that would interest travelers, such as the walls of the city.

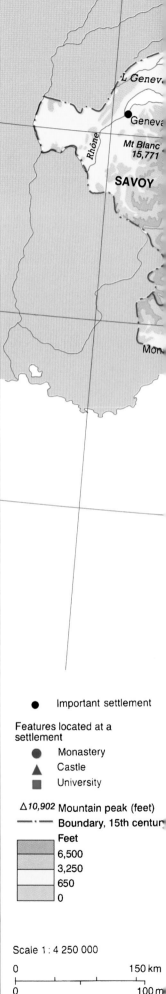

- ● Important settlement

Features located at a settlement
- ● Monastery
- ▲ Castle
- ■ University

- △10,902 Mountain peak (feet)
- —·— Boundary, 15th century

Feet
	6,500
	3,250
	650
	0

Scale 1 : 4 250 000

0   150 km

0   100 m

A   B

ALPS

Maggiore a

Como
• Como

L di Como

L di Garda

• Belluno

VENICE

• Treviso

Vicenza •

Venice •

Gulf of Venice

Chioggia

• Capo d'Istria

Vercelli •

Po

Ticino

Milan •

Brescia •
Crema •

Mantua •

Po

Turin •
• Asti
Piacenza •

Parma •

MODENA

Modena •

Ferrara •

FERRARA

• Pola

VENICE

uzzo

MILAN

Genoa •

GENOA

Bologna •

Ravenna •
VENICE

• Zadar

VENICE

• Rimini

Lucca •

Arno

Florence •

Pisa •

FLORENCE

San Gimignano •

Arezzo •

Siena •

PAPAL STATE

• Ancona

VENICE

• Split

Ligurian Sea

L Trasimeno

Perugia •

Piombino •

SIENA

Elba

L di Bolsena

Viterbo •

APENNINES

△*Mt Corno 9560*

• Chieti

Adriatic Sea

GENOA

Corsica

Tiber

○ *L di Bracciano*

Ajaccio •

• Ascoli

VENICE

• Cattaro

Rome •

Subiaco •

Sacco

• Lesina

• Lucera ▲

Fossanova •

Pontecorvo •

Volturno

• Castel del Monte ▲

Benevento •

NAPLES

Naples •

△*Mt Vesuvius 4,190*

Salerno •

Taranto •

• Brindisi

Strait of Otranto

ARAGON

Sardinia

Porto Torres •

• Policastro

Gulf of Taranto

Otranto •

Cagliari •

Tyrrhenian Sea

• Rossano

• Cosenza

2

Ionian Sea

• Squillace

Ustica

Lipari Islands

Mediterranean Sea

Palermo •

• Messina

Egadi

Reggio •

Sicily

△*Mt Etna 10,902*

Strait of Messina

ARAGON

Catania •
▲ ■

Agrigento •

Syracuse •
▲

Sicilian Channel

Pantelleria

C   D   E   F

6

5

4

3

1

San Gimignano

TODAY SOME OF THE MOST IMPRESSIVE sights in Tuscany in northern Italy are the medieval fortified towns perched on hilltops. San Gimignano is one of these, with strongly built and easily defended towers. In 12th-century Italy there were many towns such as this that were independent and controlled the lands around. Each town needed strong defenses to fight off others that might claim its territory.

Rule by the people

By the 13th century the "people"—the *popolo*— began to take over control of towns from the wealthy and powerful nobles who had run them before. The sort of people who now governed the towns were lawyers, merchants, and guilds of important industries, such as cloth manufacture.

San Gimignano was like one great castle with a wall and towers protecting the limits of the town, and all the fields outside the walls. Also important in the town at this time was the *palazzo*—the residence of the town's government.

▲ The 13th-century Palazzo del Popolo was built as the headquarters of the town's chief magistrate.

▼ San Gimignano once had 72 towers. The land around produced wine and grain as well as the spice saffron.

Florence

FLORENCE IS UNLIKE MANY OTHER TOWNS in Tuscany because it is built on a flat plain. Its position is important, as it is built on both sides of the Arno River. The river was used for defense, trade, and communications.

Florence in the 13th century

Florence became very important in the 13th century because of the industries it developed. The town was famous for its clothmaking, and the products were exported not only to other towns in Italy but also to France.

By the late 13th century the town was governed by committees made up from members of its most powerful guilds, or associations, of professions and industries. The wealth created by these industries helped pay for the building of a wall to enclose the town, begun in about 1290.

Government by the few

The richer men who lent money to the city government in the 14th century eventually took

▼ At the narrowest point of the Arno River is the Ponte Vecchio. A bridge has been here since the 10th century. This one, lined with shops, was rebuilt in 1345. It replaced one that was swept away in floods during 1333. Shops built along the side of the river emphasize the commercial importance of the river in Florence.

control of the city's affairs. Only in the 15th century did one group—the Medici—become the ruling family. Florence, which was already wealthy, began to conquer other major towns nearby, such as Arezzo in 1385 and Pisa in 1406.

The buildings of Florence

Florence was just as famous for its art and its architecture as it was for its trade and industries. The wealth created from its industries paid for many of the fine buildings, such as the Palazzo Vecchio, which we can still see today.

It was not only architects who found employment in Florence. The town had many other artists, sculptors, masons, glaziers, painters, and goldsmiths. They helped decorate the many churches and public buildings of the city.

Schools and a university

The towns of Tuscany, Florence in particular, were well known for their schools. Standards of literacy were high, and the renowned Italian poet Dante (1265–1321), who wrote *La Divina Commedia* (The Divine Comedy), was a Florentine.

But for training in law and in medicine it was necessary to go to the greater universities, such as Bologna. In Florence from the late 14th and 15th centuries some of the leading citizens encouraged the rediscovery of Greek classics and their study.

▼ Towering above the medieval buildings of Florence is its *duomo* (cathedral). It was begun in 1296 but was not consecrated as a cathedral until 1436. It is called Santa Maria del Fiore (Saint Mary of the Flower). Two parts of the cathedral stand out above the main body of the church. The great cupola (dome) was begun in 1420, and the campanile (bell tower) covered in marble was finished in 1387.

Genoa

THE TRADING TOWN OF GENOA HAD ONE very important advantage over some of its rivals: a good natural harbor. It had new markets opened to it with the success of the First Crusade in the 11th century. The wealth from its trade allowed the town to grow and develop both its harbor and its defenses.

International trade

Genoa's position on the northwestern coast of Italy meant that trade links were developed especially

▼ The Porta Soprana, with its two towers, is part of the city wall built around Genoa in 1155.

with western Europe and Africa. Cloth was the most important import from other towns in Italy and from Germany and Spain. In return, Genoa traded dyes from the east as well as spices, perfumes, and precious stones. Genoa established trading posts in Africa as bases for its merchants.

Trading rivalries

Genoa's nearest rival was Pisa. In 1284 Genoa, whose fleet was larger and more efficient, defeated Pisa in battle and gained control of the town's trade links. Its other rival, Venice—situated on the east coast of Italy—was more difficult to beat. Venice had set up its trade links in the east very early on and had a monopoly in Constantinople. Genoa founded trading posts in Asia Minor (now Turkey) to import alum, which was needed to fix dyes in cloth.

Trade

Few communities can exist simply on what they can produce themselves. People usually have to import goods—extra food, clothes, and equipment, for example—from elsewhere. Goods might have to be brought from the next village or a nearby town. But some items have to be carried vast distances. In medieval times, areas and towns came to specialize in particular goods, such as the woolen industry in Flanders. Most important towns grew as trading centers rather than as places where goods were made—towns such as Venice, London, Bruges, and Genoa.

Protecting the trade routes

Those who traded—the merchants—had to arrange for their own goods to be fetched and protected. There were many dangers. For example, piracy was a real problem in northern Europe in the 13th century. There was no overall law to protect all Europe as there had been in the Roman period.

The great center of trade in the medieval period was the Mediterranean. The Crusades made it possible for pilgrims and merchants to travel to the east. As a result, trade developed between countries in the east and the west.

▼ European trade in the 14th century. Most trade was carried out by sea. Not all overland routes are shown, but notice how many make use of rivers. Some areas developed their natural resources (such as wine or metals) for trade, while others became centers for particular trades (such as clothmaking).

Textile making areas
- Cloth
- Linen
- Fustian (rough cotton)
- Silk

— Trade route

▼ Metalworking center
▲ Important fair
● Other settlement

Location of commodity
- ● Cotton
- ● Fruit
- ● Gold
- ● Grain
- ◆ Leather
- ◆ Spices
- ◆ Sugar
- ■ Timber
- ■ Wine
- ■ Wool

Scale 1 : 20 000 000

0   600 km

0   400 miles

Land routes and sea routes

Great fairs were held all over Europe to exchange goods. At first most trade was carried out by merchants using pack animals. This meant slow journeys with the threat of attack by robbers. It also meant that only small quantities of goods could be carried. By the 14th century ships were increasingly used for trade. Large quantities of goods, such as grain for bread, could be shipped from, say, Sicily to feed the townspeople of Bruges or Antwerp.

Trading nations

Important items of trade included cloth, timber, and some foodstuffs such as grain and wine. Two Italian towns in particular established themselves as great centers of trade. Genoa was well placed to trade both inland to northern Europe and by sea in the western and eastern Mediterranean. In addition, the government in Venice was able to use its harbors to establish many trade routes.

Throughout the eastern Mediterranean you can still see Venetian forts that helped protect their trade routes. There are many on mainland Greece and its islands, in particular on Crete.

◀ Guilds (or associations) of trades and crafts were common from the 13th century. Members of the guild of cloth merchants in Bologna, Italy, are shown here filling a street with their stalls and booths.

▼ Genoa, Italy, was one of the earliest cities known for its money changers or bankers from the 12th century. Here the bankers are counting coins to give to the town's widows and orphans.

The British Isles

MANY OF THE FIELDS AND ROADS THAT can be seen in Britain today were well established long before the Romans conquered the country in 43 C.E. Since then many different peoples have made changes to the map of Britain. The names of places, for example, can often be traced to the later invasions of Anglo-Saxon, Viking, or Norman settlers.

English boundaries established

By the 13th century England was a kingdom and could properly be called a single country. It was no longer as closely linked to France as it had been before. The king had established a parliament to advise him. The king sent for powerful people to represent different parts of the country. They came from the "shires" (regions—for example, Oxfordshire or Yorkshire) and from important towns (such as Rochester). Smaller units in the country, the ecclesiastical parishes, had been established before the Norman invasion of 1066, and they continued to run local affairs.

Royal and church lands and ports

Even at this time some lands remained totally in the hands of either the king or the church, as the map shows. Five south-coast ports, called the Cinque Ports (*cinq* is French for "five"), had special privileges and duties. They were Sandwich, Dover, Hythe, Romney, and Hastings. They provided ships for the navy in return for tax allowances.

Wales and the king

The situation in Wales was different. No one prince was strong enough to dominate the whole country. When the princes of Gwynedd in the north tried to do this they were stopped by an alliance between King Edward I of England and some of the other Welsh princes. After 1284 King Edward took over the government of Gwynedd himself and built a number of castles there.

Ireland

Although King Henry II claimed the lordship of Ireland and many Norman lords were established there, the English never gained control of the whole of the island. Very few English kings ever went there. By 1485 the English really controlled only an area known as the Pale around Dublin in the south. The boundaries of medieval Ireland underwent significant changes in more recent times.

One of the best places to see what an English medieval town was like is York in the north of the country. This is the area known as the Shambles, where wooden buildings overhang the street to gain as much floor space as possible. Most of the buildings have been restored.

▼ Ireland has been a Christian country since the fifth century. Christian crosses, like this one at Castledermot, were built in many places. This is one of 50 that still survive from before the ninth century. It is highly carved and shows the suffering of Christ.

◄ The Angel Choir inside the cathedral at Lincoln, a town of about 4,000 people in the Norman period. The cathedral was begun in the late 11th century. The Normans built four cathedrals, which were served by canons (see pages 42–43). There were already nine in Britain during the Saxon period. Lincoln Cathedral was gradually enlarged and completed in the late 14th century.

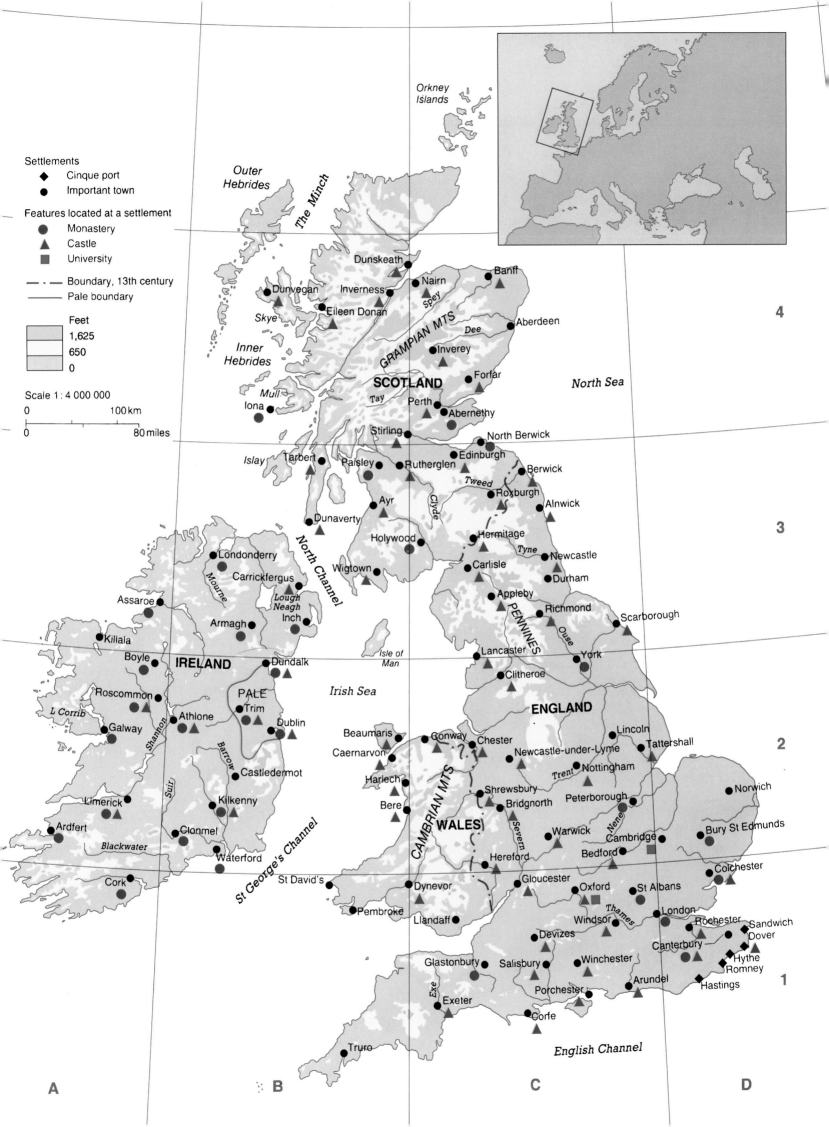

Settlements

◆ Cinque port
● Important town

Features located at a settlement

● Monastery
▲ Castle
■ University

—·—·— Boundary, 13th century
——— Pale boundary

Feet
1,625
650
0

Scale 1 : 4 000 000

0   100 km
0   80 miles

Outer Hebrides

The Minch

Orkney Islands

Dunskeath
Dunvegan
Skye
Eileen Donan
Inverness
Nairn
Spey
Banff
Aberdeen
Dee
Inverey

Inner Hebrides

GRAMPIAN MTS

Mull
Iona

SCOTLAND

Tay
Forfar
Perth
Abernethy
Stirling
North Berwick

North Sea

Islay
Tarbert
Paisley
Rutherglen
Edinburgh
Berwick
Tweed
Roxburgh
Alnwick
Ayr
Clyde
Dunaverty
Holywood
Hermitage
Tyne
Newcastle
Wigtown
Carlisle
Durham

North Channel

Londonderry
Mourne
Carrickfergus
Lough Neagh
Inch
Assaroe
Armagh
Killala
Boyle

IRELAND

Roscommon
L Corrib
Athlone
Shannon
Galway
Trim
PALE
Dublin
Dundalk

Appleby
Richmond
Scarborough
Ouse
Lancaster
York
PENNINES
Clitheroe

ENGLAND

Isle of Man

Irish Sea

Limerick
Ardfert
Suir
Barrow
Castledermot
Kilkenny
Clonmel
Blackwater
Waterford
Cork

St George's Channel

St David's
Pembroke
Llandaff

Beaumaris
Caernarvon
Gonway
Chester
Lincoln
Tattershall
Harlech
Newcastle-under-Lyme
Trent
Nottingham
Bere
Shrewsbury
Bridgnorth
Peterborough
Norwich
CAMBRIAN MTS
WALES
Severn
Warwick
Nene
Bury St Edmunds
Hereford
Cambridge
Bedford
Colchester
Dynevor
Gloucester
Oxford
St Albans
London
Rochester
Sandwich
Llandaff
Windsor
Thames
Canterbury
Dover
Devizes
Hythe
Romney
Salisbury
Winchester
Arundel
Hastings
Glastonbury
Porchester
Exe
Exeter
Corfe

English Channel

Truro

A   B   C   D

4

3

2

1

Castles

THE WORD FOR A CASTLE IN MEDIEVAL Latin was *castrum* or *castellum*. "Castle" is often used for any fortified place; the Latin word was used by the Romans for a military fort. Other, later peoples made fortifications, of course. The Saxons, for example, fortified their towns against the Danes and called them *burhs*. There is a *burh* at Dover on the southern coast of Britain, but castles of later periods have been built on top of it.

Built by the powerful

A castle was a safe place. It had to be secure against attack and a last resort for its regular inhabitants and often the people who lived around it. The site of a castle had to be carefully chosen. The best places were often already defended simply by the landscape —on a high ridge or with sheer cliffs on one side, for example. To build a castle you had to be powerful and you had to be rich.

The king often built a number of castles to hold power over the land. King Edward I of England, for example, built eight new castles in Wales between 1277 and 1304 in an attempt to control the whole of this country. However, the king could not control all his territory alone. He gave some land away to those he could trust.

In France the king granted lands and the right to control them. These were called fiefs. In return, the barons or the knights gave the king their loyalty and supplied him with fighting men.

Castles of timber and earth

In some parts of Europe the first castles built in the 10th century were made of timber (for walls, gates, and buildings inside) and earth (for the outer defenses, for example). In 11th-century England they were called motte-and-bailey castles.

A great mound (motte) of earth was constructed and a wooden building put on top. This was the keep, or strongest point, in the castle. Around it was the bailey—an area surrounded by walls of earth and timber—where the people lived. Some castles had an inner bailey (around the keep) and an outer bailey, also protected by a wall and guard towers.

Building in stone

In England after 1150 very few timber-and-earth castles were built. Stone could provide a much stronger and more permanent structure. This type of building was very expensive, however. The stone castle at Dover built in the late 12th century cost

about £7,000. That was a huge sum of money in those times. Building in stone allowed the architects to develop better ideas for making the castle a safe place to live in. At Dover the 82-foot- (25-m-) high stone keep was surrounded by a courtyard that was protected by a high wall with guard towers.

Castles were built to protect the interests of a particular lord or king or to provide a garrison for soldiers. But they were also for living in. The castle was the fortified home for the knight as well as for his family, his servants, his craftspeople, and his fighting men. In times of trouble the bailey courtyard, already full of buildings and animals, became a temporary home to surrounding villagers.

◄ Curemonte Castle in Brive la Gaillarde in France is, in fact, two castles joined by a surrounding wall with round towers built in the 14th century.

▼ Reconstruction drawing of the motte at Abinger, Surrey, in England. The mound, built by the Normans in the 11th century, had a timber watchtower on top.

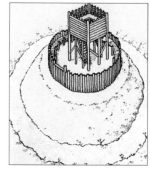

▼ The castle at Frangocastello, Crete, built by the Venetians to protect their trade routes in 1371.

▲ The Normans first built a castle at Rochester in Kent soon after the Battle of Hastings in 1066. A motte-and-bailey castle defended the crossing of the Medway River. The later stone castle on the same site and the great cathedral, seen above, were begun by Bishop Gundulf in about 1087.

▶ The keep of Rochester Castle is one of the largest in England. This huge building, with its three floors and roof battlements, was begun in 1127. There are no doors at ground level—attackers had to get past the guard tower and portcullis. On various floors there are bedrooms, halls for eating in, lavatories, and a chapel. A well inside the keep provided the occupants with fresh water.

The Countryside

TODAY IN EUROPE MOST PEOPLE GO TO THE supermarket for their daily food. Some of that food may come from the land around the town or village, but most will come from farther away or from foreign countries. By contrast, medieval people living in the countryside ate only what they produced on their own land.

In most European countries medieval kings claimed control over the land but they allowed trusted lords the rights to much of it. The lords of estates relied on tenants to work the land and collected either rents or produce each year.

Using all the land's resources

The amount of land an ordinary family was able to work varied from country to country and from place to place. In England a family with about 30 acres (12 hectares) to plow could probably live quite well from what food they could produce. Other families had to make do with considerably less.

Besides growing their crops, people had the right to graze their animals on meadows and rough land. Most people had a few animals such as sheep, pigs, and chickens and an ox or a horse for plowing. People also had the right to collect other things from the land, including turf for roofing and to burn, wood, nuts and berries, and bracken for beds and for animal food.

Hunting and fishing

For country people who were trying to survive by living off the land, the right to fish, catch eels and frogs, or net birds was essential. In some parts of

Europe hunting animals in forests provided a ready source of food and a supply of warm furs to wear and to use as bedding. Fish was an important part of the medieval diet. Monasteries, castles, and manor houses usually had their own ponds to ensure a regular supply of fresh fish.

For the wealthy, hunting was a sport that could be enjoyed. It was also an important way to keep healthy and in good shape for warfare. The hunting areas were protected and guarded against both scavenging animals and those who were not permitted to hunt. There were inhumane penalties for anybody who was caught poaching.

◀ Hunting with falcons was a popular sport for the well-born. Notice that the handlers are wearing strong leather gauntlets. The illustration comes from a book on the subject of falconry made in the mid-13th century for Manfred, King of Sicily.

▶ This illustration from a French book was made in about 1411 to illustrate the month of March. Pictures like this add to our evidence about life in the countryside gathered from archaeological work and from documents. The fields are small, and the man in the foreground is plowing with two oxen. Fields were often divided into strips and the strips allotted to the villagers so that each family had some good and some poor land to work. In the field behind, workers are pruning vines for the wine harvest.

◀ Refreshment was not forgotten after a day's hunting. This illustration and the one on the right are from *The Book of the Hunt* by Gaston Fébus, written in 1387 in France.

▶ Gaston Fébus was an expert on hunting stag and boar using dogs. He also used nets to trap hares and foxes. Nets of rope are being made here. Much finer nets were used for catching all types of birds.

Spain and Portugal

P ART OF THE STORY OF MEDIEVAL EUROPE is the struggle between two great religious faiths: Christianity and Islam. Much of this struggle took place in western Europe in the area later known as Spain and Portugal.

An Islamic Mediterranean

At the time of the death of the Islamic prophet Muhammad in 632, the Muslims controlled the area of Arabia on the eastern side of the Red Sea. Throughout the seventh century they moved north into the Holy Land and east along the Persian Gulf and Arabian Sea. They also conquered North Africa, reaching Ceuta (near Gibraltar) in 709. From here they struck out into Europe. By 750 the Muslims occupied Portugal, most of Spain, and part of southern France.

The Christians gain control

Although the Christians held a small amount of territory in the north of Spain, it was not until the middle of the 11th century that they had much success against Muslim occupation. They called this fight the *Reconquista*, or reconquest.

Most reconquest took place either in the late 11th century or in the early part of the 13th century. Land was taken away from the Muslims and given to the new conquerors. Muslims were allowed to live in the new kingdoms, at least until the 16th century, but they were forced to convert to Christianity.

Settlements
- ◆ Christian center
- ● Important town

Features located at a settlement
- ● Monastery
- ▲ Castle
- ■ University

— · — Boundary, 14th century

▼ The town of Avila in the kingdom of Castile, now Spain. Its impressive town walls were put up after the town had been reconquered from the Muslims in the late 11th century. The walls are 40 ft (12 m) high, defended by huge round towers and eight gates. The town had originally been founded by the Romans, and a lot of Roman buildings were reused to make the fortifications.

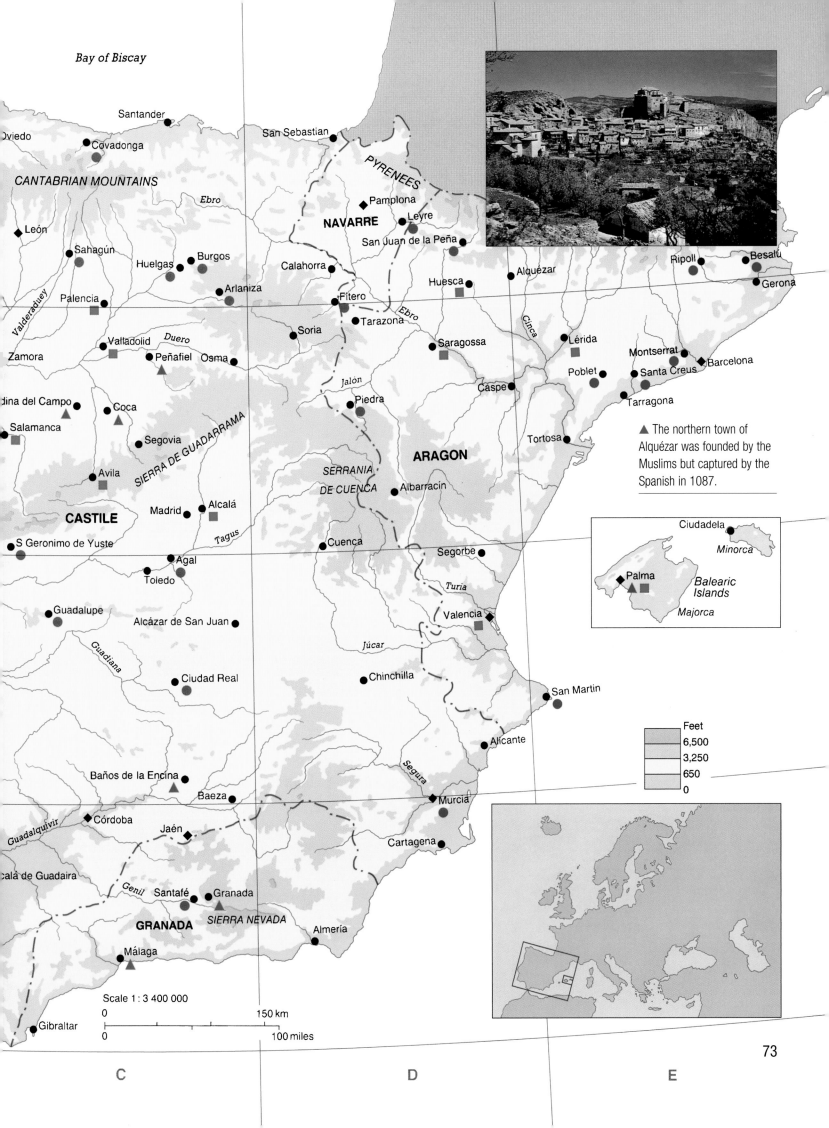

Bay of Biscay

Oviedo

Santander

Covadonga

León

CANTABRIAN MOUNTAINS

San Sebastian

PYRENEES

Pamplona

NAVARRE

Leyre

San Juan de la Peña

Sahagún

Huelgas

Burgos

Calahorra

Alquézar

Huesca

Ripoll

Besalú

Gerona

Ebro

Palencia

Arlaniza

Fitero

Ebro

Saragossa

Cinca

Lérida

Montserrat

Santa Creus

Barcelona

Valderaduey

Tarazona

Duero

Valladolid

Peñafiel

Osma

Soria

Jalón

Poblet

Tarragona

Zamora

Caspe

dina del Campo

Coca

Piedra

Tortosa

Salamanca

Segovia

SIERRA DE GUADARRAMA

▲ The northern town of
Alquézar was founded by the
Muslims but captured by the
Spanish in 1087.

Avila

ARAGON

SERRANIA
DE CUENCA

Albarracín

Ciudadela

Minorca

CASTILE

Madrid

Alcalá

Cuenca

Segorbe

Tagus

Palma

*Balearic
Islands*

S Geronimo de Yuste

Agal

Toledo

Turia

Majorca

Guadalupe

Alcázar de San Juan

Valencia

Júcar

Guadiana

Ciudad Real

Chinchilla

San Martin

Feet

Segura

Alicante

6,500

3,250

650

0

Baños de la Encina

Baeza

Murcia

Córdoba

Jaén

Cartagena

Guadalquivir

calá de Guadaira

Genil

Santafé

Granada

Almería

GRANADA

SIERRA NEVADA

Málaga

Scale 1 : 3 400 000

0   150 km

0   100 miles

Gibraltar

C

D

E

Mapmaking

THE EARLIEST MAPS WE KNOW OF IN THE world were made by the Babylonians in West Asia in about 2300 B.C.E. The Greeks also made maps, and it was to these that the first medieval mapmakers referred.

Ptolemy—Greek mapmaker

Ptolemy, an astronomer, mathematician, and geographer, was from the Greek city of Alexandria in Egypt. He wrote his work *Geography* in the second century. Copies were made in the 13th century, and the book was translated into Latin in 1406.

▼ "EVROPA MVNDI PARS QVARTA"—"Europe a quarter of the world." Part of a book written in Latin in about 1120, called *Liber Floridus*. The author thought that the world was divided into four quarters of a circle.

Sea charts and atlases

Ptolemy's work—together with specially drawn maps—was printed in Italy in 1477. But there had been new detailed maps in Europe before that time, in the 13th century. They were used mainly to help with navigation at sea.

The magnetic compass had been known as an aid since the late 12th century. These sea charts, the compass, and the astrolabe (see page 48) required a knowledge of mathematics to work out the right course. The earliest atlas that survives today was made for King Charles V of France in 1375.

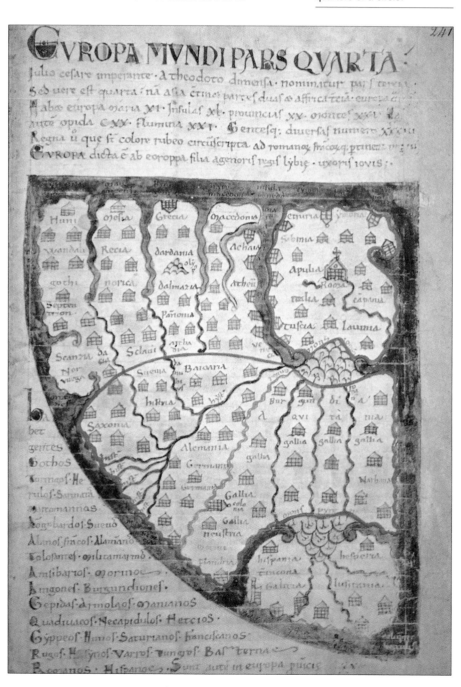

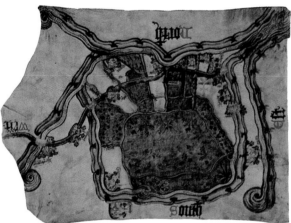

▲ A picture map of Inglemoor, England, made in 1405. It shows points of the compass, rivers, bridges, villages, fields, and the moor itself in the center. It was drawn for a court hearing when ownership of the land was disputed.

Specialized maps

Specialized maps and charts were produced in the 14th century for traders from centers in Italy such as Venice and Genoa. The Mediterranean world was very well mapped. For example, in 1320 Marino Sanudo from Venice wrote about the problem of conquering the Holy Land from the Muslims and sent his book to the Pope with a set of maps made by Pietro Visconte.

Maps of the world

In the 15th century the invention of printing meant that maps could easily be produced from woodcuts or from copper plates. It was during this century that voyages of discovery were made, and so new maps of the wider world had to be produced. Portugal led the European world in sea exploration at this time, across seas that had never before been charted.

▼ This sea chart of part of western Europe was made in 1497 by Freducci d'Ancona. Each country is recognizable today, and the coastlines have been accurately plotted. Compare this map with the modern one of Europe on pages 8–9. Here the interior of the countries is not plotted in detail—for example, Paris and London are not shown.

◄ Cartographers (map- and chartmakers) at work on a coastline from their ship. The west coast of Africa was plotted by a cartographer from Venice in 1448, but the Portuguese captains sent out by Prince Henry the Navigator had reached this coast 17 years before.

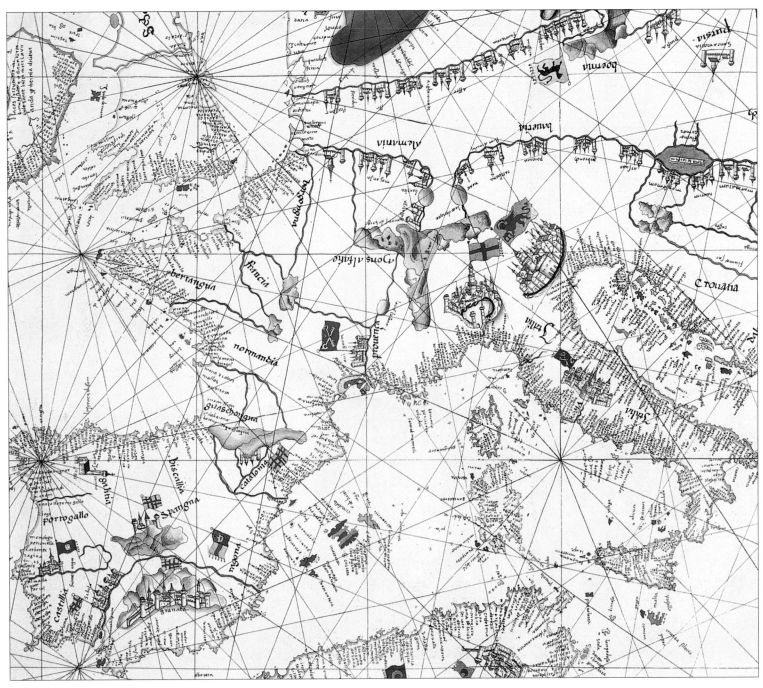

Journey to Compostela

PILGRIMAGES WERE VERY POPULAR IN medieval Europe. People so treasured the remains and possessions of the many saints that they believed they could be healed by them. Pilgrims also made their long journeys in the hope that their sins would be forgiven.

Dangerous journeys

Many pilgrims probably thought that the danger of long-distance travel was punishment enough for their sins. Jerusalem was one place that was much visited, but when the Muslims conquered the city in 638, other shrines became popular. From the 11th century parties of pilgrims were organized, such as the one described in Chaucer's *Canterbury Tales* to the shrine of murdered archbishop St. Thomas à Becket.

The shrine of St. James

The more important shrines were those of the Apostles of Christ. People believed that the tomb discovered in about 830 at Compostela in northern Spain was that of St. James the Apostle. A church was built there, and pilgrims from Spain began making the journey. The news of the shrine soon spread. At the end of the 11th century the pope ordered the bishop of the region Iria to move his headquarters there.

There were four main pilgrim routes from France to Compostela, although people also came there from farther away. Along the routes monasteries were built, and villages and towns became wealthy from the pilgrim trade.

▶ Three of the main pilgrim routes across France came together at Ostabat. In medieval times the town was very prosperous and catered to large numbers of travelers. Now Ostabat is a quiet village.

▶ This church at Conques, France, was built in the mid-11th century on the route from Le Puy to Ostabat. At Conques a local child saint was revered—St. Foy.

▼ At Santillana, on the northern coast of Spain, this church was built in the Romanesque style. This style of architecture was popular in the late 11th and 12th centuries and copied ideas from Rome.

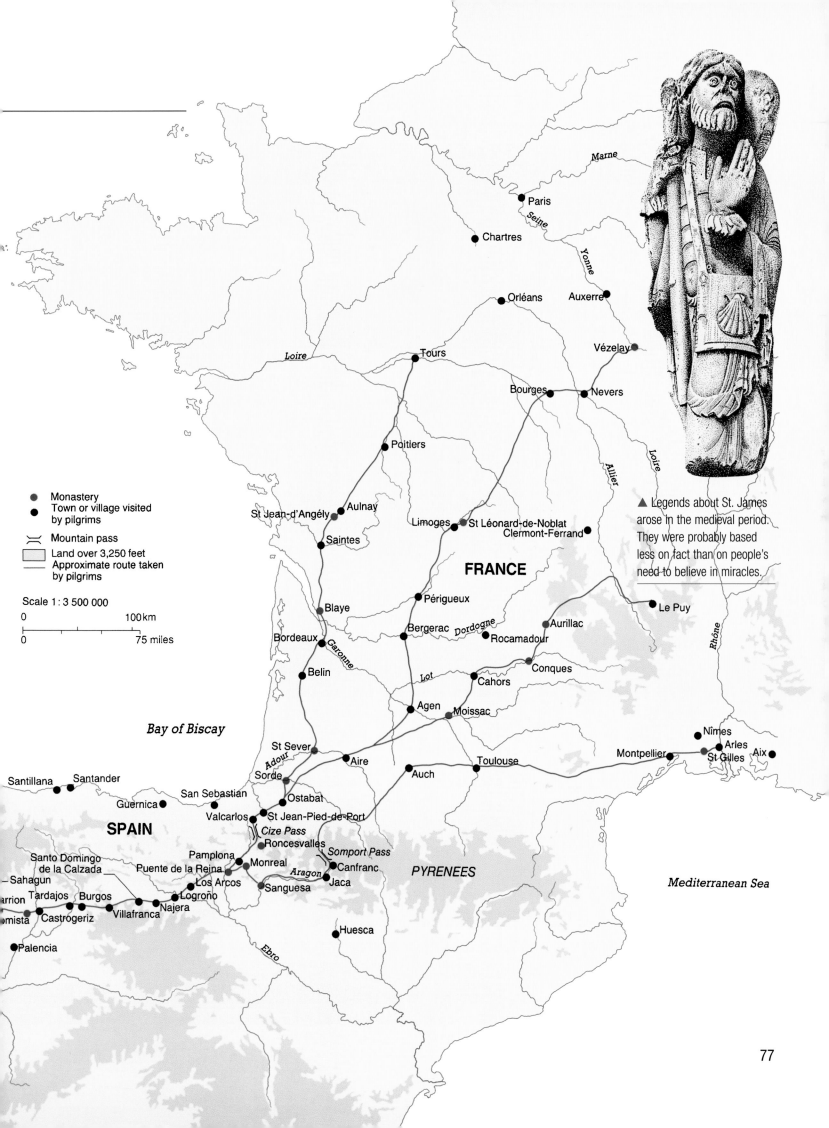

Monastery
Town or village visited by pilgrims
Mountain pass
Land over 3,250 feet
Approximate route taken by pilgrims

Scale 1 : 3 500 000

0   100km
0   75 miles

▲ Legends about St. James arose in the medieval period. They were probably based less on fact than on people's need to believe in miracles.

Marne

Seine

Paris

Chartres

Yonne

Orléans   Auxerre

Vézelay

Loire   Tours

Bourges   Nevers

Allier   Loire

Poitiers

St Jean-d'Angély   Aulnay

Limoges   St Léonard-de-Noblat
                    Clermont-Ferrand

Saintes

FRANCE

Blaye   Périgueux   Le Puy

Bordeaux   Bergerac   Dordogne   Aurillac
          Garonne   Rocamadour

                              Conques
Belin   Lot   Cahors

                    Agen   Moissac

Bay of Biscay   Nîmes
                                          Arles
St Sever   Montpellier   St Gilles   Aix
Adour   Aire
Sorde   Auch   Toulouse

Santillana   Santander
          San Sebastian
Guernica   Ostabat   Mediterranean Sea
Valcarlos   St Jean-Pied-de-Port
SPAIN   Cize Pass
            Roncesvalles   Somport Pass
Pamplona   Monreal   Canfranc   PYRENEES
Santo Domingo Puente de la Reina   Jaca
de la Calzada   Aragon
Sahagun   Los Arcos   Sanguesa
arrion Tardajos Burgos Logroño
mista Castrogeriz Villafranca Najera
Palencia   Huesca

Ebro

77

Central Europe

SOME PARTS OF MEDIEVAL EUROPE developed quite separate histories, which were not connected with the establishment of the large Roman Empire. However, the German Empire, or Holy Roman Empire, looked back to Rome and tried to reestablish some of its traditions.

Development of an empire

"The Empire," as it was known, was not completely controlled by one emperor. The 14th century was a period of great change in medieval Europe, and in the German Empire a number of families held power. Two families in particular ruled the Empire: the Luxembourg family from 1346 to 1437 and then the Hapsburgs from 1438 onward. However, a number of separate states and cities that declared themselves "free" also made up the Empire.

Governing a large territory

Some noble families claimed the throne of the Empire, and wars frequently went on between powerful groups. However, the emperor had to be elected by princes and had to influence them and the independent cities and states in order to remain in overall control.

Switzerland

This area in particular shows the complicated way in which the Empire was formed and governed. Switzerland had been part of the territory of the German Empire since the 11th century and was ruled by a number of noble families.

During the 13th century the number of Swiss towns rose from 16 to 80. In 1291 a confederation of independent districts and prosperous towns joined together. Their independence showed that Switzerland was powerful and not afraid to use its army to resist the German princes. Switzerland was nevertheless part of the German Empire.

The Low Countries

Another example of the complicated nature of the Empire can be seen in the countries that bordered the North Sea (present-day Belgium and the Netherlands). Flanders had been part of the French kingdom but passed into the territory of the dukes of Burgundy, who also took over Brabant in 1404. In fact, by the middle part of the 15th century the dukes of Burgundy had become very rich and powerful. They held land from the Swiss border north to Holland and built up Antwerp as a trading port.

▲ The 12th-century bridge across the Danube River at Regensburg, Germany.

▶ Toplerschlösschen im Rosenthal. The fortified German tower guards the town's mills.

▼ Rothenburg's walls were rebuilt in the 14th century.

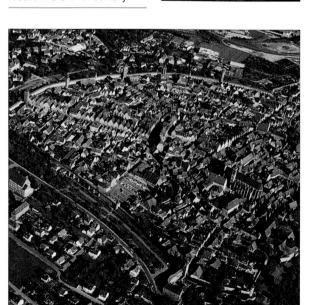

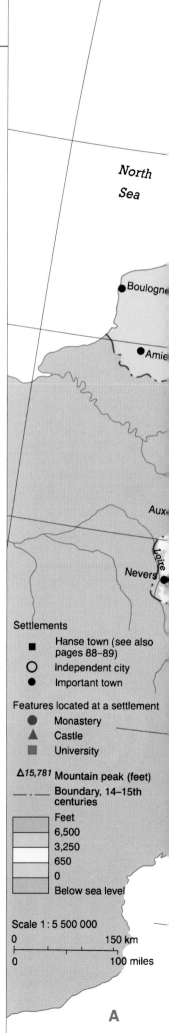

North Sea

● Boulogne

● Amie

Aux

Nevers

Settlements

■ Hanse town (see also pages 88–89)

○ Independent city

● Important town

Features located at a settlement

● Monastery

▲ Castle

■ University

△15,781 Mountain peak (feet)

—·—·— Boundary, 14–15th centuries

Feet
6,500
3,250
650
0
Below sea level

Scale 1 : 5 500 000

0 — 150 km

0 — 100 miles

A

Baltic Sea

6

Kiel

Rostock   Greifswald

Ritzebüttel   Lübeck

Groningen   Hamburg   Stettin

Oldenburg   Bremen   Elbe

Havelberg

Deventer   Aller   5

Utrecht   Osnabrück   Hanover   Brandenburg   Frankfurt

Münster   Herford   Goslar

Antwerp   Dortmund   Paderborn   Quedlinburg   Breslau

Essen   **GERMAN   EMPIRE**   Leipzig

ssels   Louvain   Cologne   Erfurt   Meissen   Luban   SUDENTEN MTS

brai   Aix   Marburg   Zeitz   Königingrätz

Stablo   Fulda   Weser   Prague

ARDENNES   Rhine   Koblenz   Olomouc

Moselle   Frankfurt   Schweinfurt   Waldsassen   Vltava   Brünn

hel   Trier   Heidelberg   Würzburg

Luxembourg   Toplerschlösschen im Rosenthal   **BOHEMIAN**   4

Bar   Speyer   Rothenburg   Regensburg   Budweis

Metz   Trifels   Gmünd   Nördlingen   Ingolstadt   **FOREST**

Strasbourg   Tübingen   Augsburg   Passau

VOSGES   Alpirsbach   Munich   Danube   Vienna

MTS   Buchau   Waidhofen

Münster   **BLACK**   Danube   Salzburg

Luxeuil   **FOREST**   Rhine   Constance

Basle   Lindau   Inn

Doubs   Besançon   Zurich

Beaune   Innsbruck   Grossglockner   Mur   3

Saône   **JURA MTS**   Berne   Chur   12,461   Gurk

Lausanne   Disentis   Brixen   **DOLOMITES**   Drava

on   L Geneva   Sierre   **ALPS**   L Maggiore   Adige

Rhône   Geneva   Trent   Sava

Mt Blanc   △Matterhorn   L di Como   Gorizia

15,771   14,692   Como   Po

Aosta   L di Garda

Rhône   Milan   Vicenza   2

Durance   Turin   Piacenza   Po

Arles   Modena   **Adriatic**

Aix   Genoa   **APENNINES**   **Sea**

Ligurian

Monaco   Arno   Florence   **Sea**

Pisa

Siena

Mediterranean Sea   1

B   C   D

Everyday Life

FOR VERY MANY PEOPLE IN MEDIEVAL Europe life was hard—perhaps harder for those living in towns than for those in the countryside. Despite much poverty and disease, the population rose quickly. We think that there were about 22.5 million inhabitants of western Europe in 950. By the middle of the 14th century, the number had doubled.

Towns

Although most people lived in the country, more towns grew up in the medieval period. By today's standards they were not very big. The larger towns, such as Hamburg and London, each had between 20,000 and 40,000 inhabitants by the 14th century.

There were more than 100,000 people in only a very few cities, such as Paris, Milan, and Venice. Town and countryside were not separated in quite the same way as they are today. Many townspeople cultivated gardens and fields and kept animals inside the town's walls.

Evidence about everyday life

While we have some evidence about the lives of ordinary people from documents and pictures, we can also find out a great deal from the results of archaeological work. For example, we can look at leather shoes that were preserved by being thrown into a well when they were worn out.

Everyone in the medieval world used pottery to store things in, to cook with, and to eat from. Pottery fragments survive very well. Some of the most interesting evidence comes from wooden carvings, often found on church seats, which were being made as early as the 13th century.

Industry

Industry was usually carried out in towns. Specialized workshops (not factories) were established, often in the place where the raw material was found. For example, we know that there was pottery production in Cologne in Germany by at least the eighth century. Much of the work was done by hand. Craftsmen carved animal bone and horn into everyday objects such as counters for games, combs, buttons, and even ice skates. But machines were introduced where possible, to help with production. Spinning wheels and clocks were both medieval inventions. In the countryside wind- and watermills provided power. Watermills were used for sawing wood, making cloth, and making paper.

▲ Humorous wooden carving from the church at Fairford, England, showing a husband being battered by his wife. It is on a misericord, or "mercy seat"—a ledge cut under a tip-up seat to allow the clergy to take the weight off their feet during long church services.

◀ Inside a German kitchen the housewife or housekeeper cooks over a wood fire. In the iron cauldron is the daily pottage, or soup-stew, made from vegetables and meat.

▼ ▶ Guilds often paid for stained-glass windows in churches (right). A drapers' (clothmakers') guild had these made. They show a man carding (combing) the cloth and cutting the nap (the rough surface).

There were many small industries in towns, places for shops and where goods could be traded (below). This scene is of a German town in the early 16th century.

Guilds

Often groups of specialized workers formed themselves into guilds, made up from masters who ran the shops of workmen. Each guild laid down rules for the way they worked, traded, and trained new workers (the apprentices).

The rules of the guild always stressed the importance of the members' religious duties. Like similar associations today, they also looked after their members and their members' families in times of trouble or hardship. Guilds played an important part in the running and government of some towns and could be very powerful.

Southeastern Europe

THE AREA COVERED IN THE MAP ON THE right is vast—roughly 11 times the size of England. The history of this area in the medieval period is the most complicated in Europe. There were two main aspects to this history. One was the continuing involvement in this area of western European kings, states, and cities. The other was the gradual increase in the size of the Muslim Empire under the Ottoman Turks.

The Ottoman threat
The Ottoman Turks at the beginning of the 14th century held only a small amount of land on the southern edge of the Black Sea. Through the 14th and 15th centuries they were able to gain control of Asia Minor, Greece, and part of the Balkans. They took Constantinople, which had been the capital of the East Roman Empire, in 1453. These Muslim Turks were dedicated soldiers. Their huge and effective armies had little difficulty in overcoming the divided forces of the western European princes who opposed them.

Greece and the Balkans
There were many groups in this area to fight the Muslim advance, but often they fought each other as well. The Order of the Knights of St. John defended the island of Rhodes against the Muslims. The Venetians and the Genoese held territory in Greece and Asia Minor. Their occupation held back the Muslims, but these two cities were more interested in trade than in establishing a new Christian empire in the east. For much of the 14th century, in fact, they fought each other.

Other western groups were interested in this part of the world, but their military power was limited. The king of Aragon acquired Sicily in 1282, and then in the 14th century Catalans took Athens and a large area around it. For a time the French controlled some lands in Greece and northward as far as Hungary. The situation changed often.

Bohemia
To the north of the area fought over by Muslims and Christians was the powerful kingdom of Bohemia. The mountains of Bohemia provided Europe with much of its basic supplies of gold and silver. The Czechs, Bohemia's most influential people, were ruled by their own kings until the 14th century. By then the king of Bohemia held the most important position in central Europe.

◀ The finely decorated west front of the abbey at Ják in western Hungary. This is 13th-century architecture, dating from the rebuilding of the abbey after the invasion of the Mongol hordes in 1241.

Bohemia took over a number of neighboring states, including Hungary to the south and Lausitz to the north. The ruler of the German Empire was elected by the king of Bohemia and six German princes. At one time in the early 14th century the kings of Bohemia even ruled Poland. The first university of the German Empire was founded in Prague in 1348.

▼ The castle and defensive walls of the Knights of St. John on the island of Rhodes. Between 1310 and 1522 the knights, driven out from Acre in the Holy Land, crusaded against the Muslims from Rhodes.

Luckau

LAUSITZ

Glogow

Luban

Breslau

Oder

SUDENTEN

SILESIA

Eger

Prague

Elbe

Konigingratz

Raciborz

BOHEMIA

Olomouc

Klatovy

Iglau

Zilina

Vltava

Budweis

Bratislava

Nitra

Saros

Lelesz

Danube

Eger

Szatmar

Esztergom

Ofen

Ják

HUNGARIAN

Oradea

L Balaton

HUNGARY

Cluj

MOLDAVIA

PLAIN

Kalocsa

Siret

Siretul

Iasi

CARPATHIAN MTS

Pécs

Drava

Gyulafehervar

Mures

Zagreb

Csanad

Akkerman

Sava

Djakovo

Focsani

Senj

TRANSYLVANIAN ALPS

Kilia

Dubica

Armenis

Danube

DALMATIA

Belgrade

Tumu Severin

WALLACHIA

Zadar

DINARIC ALPS

Morava

Bucharest

Srebrehica

Vidin

Danube

Silistria

Sarajevo

Sibenik

Split

Nis

BULGARIA

Black Sea

BOSNIA

Durmitor△ 8274

Novi Pazar

Iskür

Varna

Sofia

BALKAN MTS

Important settlement

Dubrovnik

Pec

△Musala 9,596

Burgas

Features located at a settlement

MONTE-NEGRO

SERBIA

Plovdiv

Monastery

Bar

L Shkoder

Skopje

BYZANTINE EMPIRE

Castle

Durazzo

Melnik

RHODOPE MTS

Adrianople

University

Ochrida

Struma

Constantinople

Nicomedia

△ 9,570 Mountain peak (feet)

Ohridsko L

Prespa L

Sea of Marmara

Boundary, 14th century

Vlore

Thessalonica

Thasos

Gallipoli

Bursa

Sakarya

Feet

Aliakmon

GREECE

Karies

OTTOMAN EMPIRE

6,500

Mt Olympos 9,570

Lemnos

ASIA MINOR

3,250

Meteora

Larisa

Aegean Sea

650

Corfu

Lesbos

Phocaea

0

Corfu

PINDUS MTS

Andinitsa

Euboea

Chios Volissos

Ionian Is

GREECE

ATHENS

Karistos

Patras

Athens

Andros

ACHAEA

Argos

Idra

Naxos

Modon

GREECE

Mistra

DUCHY OF

Kos

Rhodes

NAXOS

Cerigo

Rhodes

Scale 1 : 8 000 000

Crete

Candia

0   200 km

Frangocastello

0   150 miles

A   B   C

Northeastern Europe

THE TWO MOST IMPORTANT STATES IN THE far eastern part of medieval Europe were Poland and Russia. In between these two great states stood Lithuania, which emerged as a separate state in the 13th century and by the end of the 14th century was combined with Poland under a Lithuanian king.

Poland

The name Poland comes from a Slavonic word, *pole*, meaning a field or plain. Its people were *poleni*—the inhabitants of the fields. Unlike in other areas of medieval Europe, here the territories controlled by tribes were joined together as a state quite early on in history. Poland's first ruler was Mieszko I, who governed from 963 to 992. Soon after he took over he was converted to Christianity, and Poland became a Catholic state accepting the authority of the pope in Rome.

Mieszko established the Piast dynasty (but the name of this ruling family was not applied to the dynasty until the 17th century), although he had to pay homage to the powerful German emperor.

▼ Krakow in Poland was an important city in the development of the country. It became the headquarters (called the "seat") of the bishop in about 1000. The cathedral shown here was built in about 1018 but rebuilt in the 14th century. Krakow University was established in 1364.

Poland did not survive long as one unified state. In the 12th century the land was ruled by a number of dukes but was reunited in the 14th century.

Russia

The land we know today as Russia developed in quite a different way. In the 10th century the cities around Kiev were linked together under the rule of descendants of merchant-soldiers who had come from Scandinavia. For a long time communities whose wealth came from agriculture not trade ruled themselves, but they were overrun by the Mongol hordes from the east in the early 13th century.

After this the Russians were divided into two main groups—the Great Russians and the White Russians. The Great Russians, whose power base was the growing city of Moscow, emerged as the stronger group in the 13th and 14th centuries.

▲ Icons (images of God, Christ, and the saints) were important in Russian Orthodox Christianity. This icon was made in the 14th century in western Russia, and shows the Trinity with God, the child Christ, and the dove of the Holy Spirit.

Important settlement

Features located at a settlement
- Monastery
- University

—··— Boundary, 14th century

Feet
3,250
650
0

Scale 1 : 9 000 000
0   200km
0   150 miles

Baltic Sea

Marienwalde
Poznan
Warthe   Plock
Wschowa
Lodz
POLAND
Radomsko
Krakow
Stary Sac

A

Lake Onega

Kargopol

Velikii Ustyug

Lake Ladoga

Sukhona

Gulf of Finland

Neva

Staroladozhskii

Ferapontov

Oreshek

Blagoveschenskii

Kirov

Volkhov

Vologda

RUSSIA

Galich

Shcheremenskii

Novgorod

Borovich

Krasnokholmskii

Unzha

Lovat

Yaroslavl

Volga

Nikolaevskii Tikhonov

Kholm

Rostov

Gorodets

Torzhok

Volga

Tver

Suzdal

Nizhnii Novgorod

Volga

Braslav

Dvina

Moscow

Murom

Polotsk

Gzhatsk

Neman

CENTRAL

Vilna

Dnieper

Smolensk

RUSSIAN

Oka

Ryazan

Grodno

Minsk

Kirov

Don

Novogrudok

Mogilev

UPLANDS

Kaluga

Odoyev

Wizna

Dankov

LITHUANIA

Yelets

arsaw

Brest

Pripet

arka

Turov

Lublin

Desna

Wlodximierz

Chernigov

Lutsk

Lvov

Kiev

Halicz

Bjelgorod

Poltava

Dniester

Bug

Dnieper

B

C

D

4

3

2

1

A Russian Village

T HE SCENE BELOW OF A MEDIEVAL VILLAGE in Russia has been reconstructed from a number of different sources. Some buildings survive, and there are drawings in manuscripts that also have written descriptions of village life.

Setting the scene

It was not until very recently that people living in towns and country villages could avoid the mud and slush caused by unpaved roads. In winter the stoves in the houses provided the only warmth.

Buildings of wood

Medieval houses all across Europe were built using wood. But Russian villages and towns were built almost completely of wood—even Moscow, which became known as the Wooden City. Split tree trunks were laid to make the tracks usable.

The houses were made of logs, and fire was the greatest hazard. Here, the chapel is also constructed from wood, even the roof. There was a great deal of very elaborate wood carving on some buildings, as on the little dome in our illustration. The cross standing on its own is also made of wood.

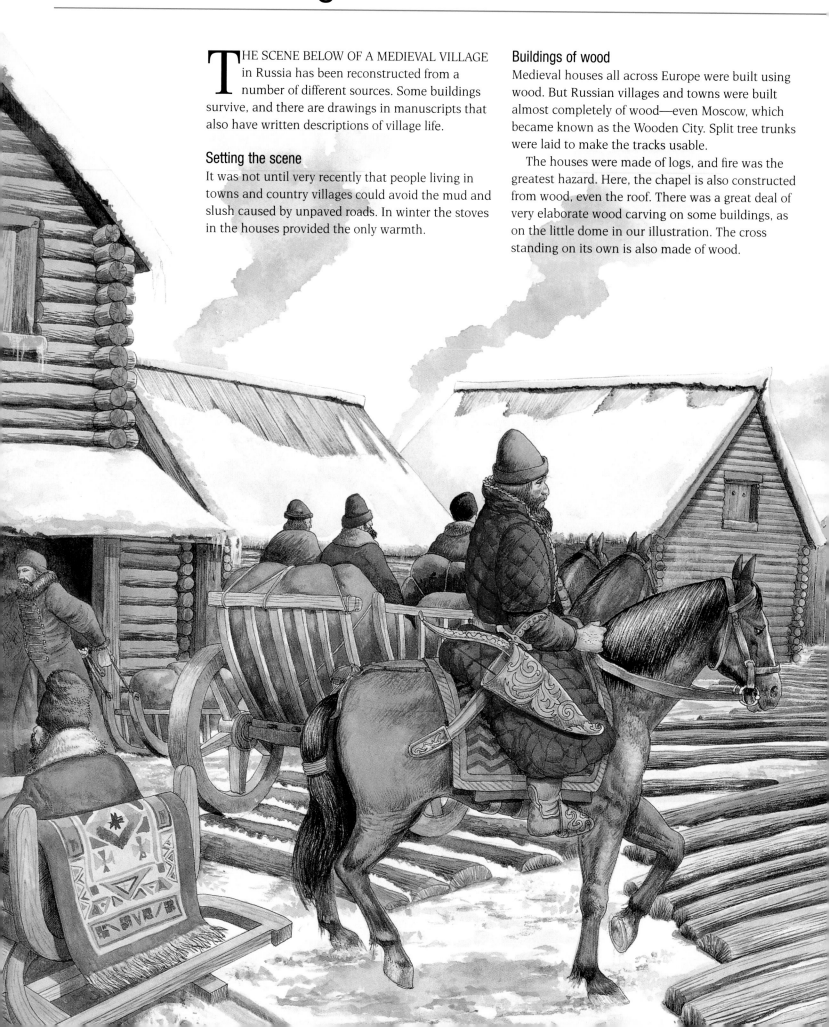

▼ In this scene, the *boyar's* weapons and the means of transport were inherited from the Mongols. As skilled warrior horsemen, the Mongols overran northern China, north India, and Russia as far west as the Black Sea. Their influence in Russia lasted until the end of the medieval period.

People and travel

It was obviously difficult to travel in such conditions. In Russia the sled was very useful, especially over frozen ground and iced-over rivers. In the illustration, the central figure on horseback is a *boyar*—originally the title meant a leader of a tribe, but it was later used for a nobleman who owned land. Between the chapel and the cross stands a bearded priest.

87

Scandinavia

WE HAVE SEEN EARLIER (PAGES 24–25) how the early peoples of northern Europe—the Vikings— moved out from Scandinavia. They invaded foreign countries and settled far afield.

England and Scandinavia

In the 11th century under King Canute the histories of England and Scandinavia were connected. King Canute of England became king of Denmark in 1016 after his brother Harold died. He then moved into Norway in 1028. This military occupation was followed by Anglo-Saxon priests who converted people to Christianity and built churches.

By the 12th century Denmark had become a power in its own right and later conquered Norway and moved north toward Finland.

Sweden

In the 13th century the Scandinavian peoples were not a unified group. In Sweden a number of great nobles ruled the country. Under one of them, Jarl Birger, in the mid-13th century, southern Finland was conquered.

Trading towns and the Baltic

The Vikings had established a number of trading posts, usually heavily fortified, in the Baltic. By the 12th century trade was in the hands of about 200 German towns which formed together into an association or league called the Hanse (the word meant a fellowship) to protect their mutual trading interests. Trading methods were made more efficient by the introduction of bookkeeping and buying and selling on credit rather than exchange. The first center for the Hanse was at Gothland (Wisby), but this was transferred to Lübeck, Germany, in the mid-13th century.

By the 15th century the power of the Hanse declined for three reasons. Firstly, the Scandinavian countries joined together; secondly, the size of the herring shoals in the North Sea were declining; and thirdly, trade was shifting to the Atlantic coasts.

Traded goods

Foreign agencies were established in England, France, Russia, and Norway. Items of trade included fish, wine (from France and Germany), cattle (from Hungary and Poland), furs (from Russia), metals and wood (from Sweden), butter and cattle (from Denmark), and wool (from England).

▲ Detail from a 12th-century tapestry in a church in Skog, a small town north of Stockholm, Sweden. The tapestry depicts the struggle between Christianity and paganism that took place at this time throughout much of Scandinavia.

◄ The testing of the sword— a detail of a 12th-century carving from a stave church portal illustrating the story of Sigurd, a hero of Norse mythology. The church is in Hylestad, about 160 miles (257 km) southeast of Bergen, Norway.

Settlements

- ■ Hanse town (see also pages 78–79)
- ● Important town

Features located at a settlement
- ● Monastery
- ▲ Castle

- △ 6,926 Mountain peak (feet)
- –·–·– Boundary, 12th century (where known)

Feet
- 6,500
- 3,250
- 650
- 0

Scale 1 : 7 500 000

| 0 | | 200 km |
| 0 | | 150 miles |

Norwegian Sea

Lofoten Islands

Kebnekaise △ 6,926

Torne

Lule

L Imari

Kemi

L Storaven

Ströms Vattudal

Ume

Gulf of Bothnia

L Olujarvi

● Trondheim

NORWAY

● Skog

FINLAND

L Saimaa

SWEDEN

L Nasijarvi

Glittertind △ 8,087

Sognefjorden

● Søgne

Glama

Ljusan

Klar

Lake Ladoga

● Bergen

Lagen

● Hamar

Vyborg ●

● Stavanger

● Hylestad

● Oslo

● Tonsberg

● Uppsala

Vasteras ●

L Malaren

Birka ■ Stockholm ▲

● Turku

● Helsinki

Gulf of Finland

L Vanern

● Skara

● Linkoping

Gotland

Skagerrak

● Kungaly

L Vattern

■ Wisby ▲

● Ålborg

● Varberg

DENMARK

● Vaxjo

● Viborg

● Kalmar ▲

● Aarhus

Oland

● Halsingborg

Baltic Sea

● Ribe

● Roskilde

● Copenhagen

● Malmö

● Svendborg

● Flensburg

● Schleswig

■ Kiel

● Trelleborg

5

4

3

2

1

A

B

C

Søgne

ALTHOUGH THE FIRST CHRISTIAN KING OF Norway was Håkon "the Good" in the mid-10th century, there had been Christians in Scandinavia long before that time. Archaeological evidence for Christianity comes from burials and stone monuments found in the countryside. Churches must have been built by the missionaries in the ninth and 10th centuries, but no remains have been found so far. Any such churches were almost certainly built of wood.

Stave churches

Stave churches—made using wooden planks cut from split logs—were built in Scandinavia to a simple plan. There was usually a rectangular nave and a square chancel with four central posts to hold up the roofs. Some of the churches had aisles. Outside, though, these churches were often very elaborate. Borgund church, shown below, has a series of roofs with complicated and detailed carvings of animals' heads.

▼ Borgund church, Søgne, in western Norway, was built in about 1150. The whole church, including the roof tiles, was built of wood. Between 1000 and 1300 all churches in Norway were wooden—about 700 in all. Today only 25 still stand.

Trelleborg

THE SITE OF TRELLEBORG IN WEST Sjaelland, Denmark, is the best-preserved example we have of a Viking fortress. It was built and occupied between the middle of the 10th and the early 11th centuries, one of four very similar circular fortresses. These huge fortresses are unique in western Europe, although some people have suggested that the idea came from two of the Vikings' enemies—the Slavs (of central and eastern Europe) and the Saxons (of Germany).

We know quite a lot about Trelleborg because the site was extensively excavated in the 1930s.

Built to a careful plan

Like the other fortresses, Trelleborg must have been authorized by the king of Denmark. All four fortresses are built to a similar plan. They are round and divided inside into four regular quadrants, marked out by streets that cross the fortresses. The buildings, each of the same type, were set out inside the quadrants in fours around a courtyard. The layout of the fortresses and the buildings is based on a Roman measurement—the foot. The fortress at Trelleborg housed approximately 500 Vikings—about the size of a large town at the time.

Solid defenses

Excavations at Trelleborg have shown that the defenses there are of earth with a wooden structure inside. Wooden palisades (fences) held this outer rampart together. At each of the four entrances there were large, heavy timber gates and guard towers. Beyond that was a ditch. Unlike the other fortresses, Trelleborg has another rampart running around it for extra protection.

Barracks and workshops

The buildings inside are all made of wood, with the roofs either thatched (as shown here) or covered in wooden tiles (called shingles). They are long, with the posts of the timber frames of the buildings set into the ground. These long buildings must have been barrack blocks for the troops.

Excavations have also shown that there was a variety of small industrial workshops—such as for metalworking—on the site. It is possible that the taxes collected for the king were stored inside this heavily protected fortress.

▶ The fortress at Trelleborg differs from the other three in that it had an annex (top right). The annex, which is protected by its own double rampart and ditches, contains 13 more buildings of the same type as those inside the fortress.

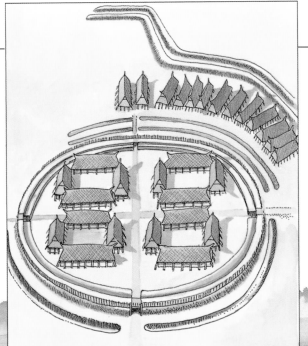

▼ One corner of the fortress at Trelleborg shows the buildings in more detail. The rampart around the outside is built at two levels for strength and to allow access for guards. Each group of buildings may have had several uses—as barracks, as housing for local people in times of trouble, or as centers of royal administration.

Glossary

aisle Part of a church, usually added at the sides of the nave, with its roof supported by columns.

archaeologists People who work carefully, like detectives, to uncover the remains of the past, sometimes excavating for evidence, sometimes recording buildings or other structures.

bailey The area of a castle, enclosed by an outer wall, in which the people lived.

barbarians or barbari The word used by the Romans for any foreigner living beyond their boundaries who did not speak Latin.

barrow A mound of earth heaped up over a burial.

caliph The title of the ruler of Islam after the prophet Muhammad.

canon A clerk who lived according to holy rules.

castle A strongly fortified place built by the king or a local lord or ruler to protect their lands and to provide a safe place for themselves, their families, and retainers.

cathedral The main church of a bishop.

chancel The part of the church where the priest conducts the service.

chapter house The place in a monastery where the daily meetings of the religious community were held.

Cinque Ports The name originally given to five ports on the south coast of England that were granted special privileges in return for certain duties.

clinker-built boats Boats made from overlapping timber planks.

condottieri Mercenary soldiers in 14th- and 15th-century Italy.

crusade A religious war to win back the Holy Lands from non-Christians. The word comes from the habit of sewing crosses on to the soldiers' clothing.

diocese Term originally used for a district of the late Roman Empire. It is later used as a smaller district controlled by a bishop.

Domesday Book A record of property and its owners in England ordered by King William I in 1086 C.E.

earthworks A term used by archaeologists to describe any remains (of earth) that can be seen on the surface of the ground.

East Roman Empire That part of the Roman Empire centered on the city of Constantinople (also known as Byzantium, now as Istanbul). *See also* West Roman Empire. Also called the Byzantine or Holy Christian Empire.

empire A very large territory, usually covering more than one country, ruled by an emperor.

fief Land granted by the king in return for military service.

flying buttresses Supports of arches built on the outside of cathedrals to carry the enormous weight of the high roofs.

fort or fortress The fortified place for a body of soldiers to live in.

guild An association of merchants or craftsmen.

Hanse A trading association or league of German towns.

hoards Collections of money or valuable goods that were buried or hidden in troubled times but never recovered by their owners.

Islam The religion of the Muslim peoples.

keep The strongest part and last refuge of a castle. It is generally where the lord of the castle and his family lived.

knight The word originally meant an attendant. It came to mean a noble who served a king as a soldier on horseback, and who could provide arms and armor.

manuscript A piece of writing made by hand and not printed.

mercenaries Soldiers paid to fight.

militia Local troops defending Italian towns until the 14th century.

misericords or mercy seats Tip-up seats used by the clergy during long services.

monastic Term used of a cathedral where the priests were monks.

motte The mound, on which the keep usually stood, of the early timber-and-earth castles.

Muslim A believer in the Islamic religion.

nave The part of a church where the congregation stands or sits for the service.

orders Communities of monks or nuns who followed a Rule or code. There were also orders of knights established during the Crusades.

parlement Originally the place for discussion in the French kingdom that became the chief royal court of law.

parliament A group of advisers established by the king in England to advise him. It has never lost the status of the highest court in the land.

pilgrimage A journey (usually long) to visit the shrine of a saint. Pilgrims hoped their sins would be forgiven because they were making these journeys.

shrine A holy place, perhaps where the remains of a saint are kept.

West Roman Empire That part of the Roman Empire centered on Rome (*see also* East Roman Empire). It eventually became broken up into the Frankish Empire and several barbarian states.

FURTHER READING/ WEB SITES

Reference books about the medieval period

Black, M. *Food and Cooking in Medieval Britain: History and Recipes* (English Heritage, 1985).

Corbishley, M. *Timelink: The Medieval World* (Hamlyn, 1992).

Corbishley, M. *Real Castles* (English Heritage/TAG Publishing, 2000).

Caselli, G. *A Medieval Monk* (Peter Bedrick Books, 1986).

Caselli, G. *A Viking Settler* (Peter Bedrick Books, 1986).

Firth, A. Internet-linked Books of Discovery: *Knights* (Usborne, 2002).

Hinds, K. Life in the Middle Ages Series: *The City, The Castle, The Countryside, The Church* (Benchmark Books, 2000).

Holmes, G. (ed.). *The Oxford Illustrated History of Medieval Europe* (Oxford University Press, 2001).

Langley, A. DK Eyewitness Guides: *Medieval Life* (Dorling Kindersley, 1996).

Macaulay, D. *Castle* (Houghton Mifflin, 1977).

Matthew, D. *Atlas of Medieval Europe* (Facts On File, 1983).

Matthews, J. *Warriors of Christendom* (Firebird Books, 1990).

Morgan, G. *Life in a Medieval Village* (Lerner Publications, 1982).

Nardo, D. *The Middle Ages* (Lucent Books, 2002).

Nicolle, D. *See Through History: Medieval Knights* (Heinemann Library, 1997).

Sims, L. *Usborne Internet-linked Book of Castles* (Usborne, 2002).

Squire, G., and P. Baynes. *The Observer's Book of European Costume* (Warne, 1975).

Williams, B. *See Through History: Forts and Castles* (Heinemann Library, 1994).

Interactive resources and Web sites

Corbishley, M., and M. Cooper. *Real Castles: Digital Time Traveller* (Tag/English Heritage, 2000). Text with activities, CD-ROM with games, Web sites to visit.

http://www.bbc.co.uk/schools/romans
Web site of the British Broadcasting Corporation, with resources, glossary, and timeline for children.

http://www.historyforkids.org
Community service learning project from Portland State University.

http://www.jorvik-viking-centre.co.uk
Web site for the famous excavated Viking town.

http://www.newyorkcarver.com/cathedrallinks.htm
Photo tours of some of the most important Gothic cathedrals in Europe.

Gazetteer

The gazetteer lists places and features, such as islands or rivers, found on the maps. Each has a separate entry including a page and grid reference number. For example:
Alcala 73 C3

All features are shown in italic type. For example:
Andros, i. 83 B1

A letter after the feature describes the kind of feature:
i. island; *mt.* mountain; *mts.* mountains; *r.* river

Åarhus 89 B2
Aberdeen 67 C4
Abernethy 67 C4
Adrianople 83 B2
Agal 73 C2
Agen 55 C2
Agrigento 61 D1
Aisne, r. 55 C4
Aix 79 B2
Aix 79 B5
Ajaccio 61 B3
Akkerman 83 C3
Albarracin 73 D3
Albi 55 C1
Ålborg 89 B2
Alcacer do Sal 72 B2
Alcalá 73 C3
Alcalá de Guadaira 73 C1
Alcántara 72 B2
Alcázar de San Juan 73 C2
Alcobaça 72 A2
Algiers 8 C1
Alicante 73 D2
Allier, r. 8 C2, 55 C2
Almeria 73 D1
Alnwick 67 C3
Alpirsbach 79 B4
Alps, mts. 9 C2, 61 B6, 79 B3
Alquézar 73 E4
Amboise 55 C3
Amiens 78 A4
Amsterdam 8 C3
Ancona 61 D4
Andinitsa 83 B1
Andros, i. 83 B1
Angers 55 B3
Angoulême 55 C2
Ankara 9 F2
Aosta 61 B5, 79 B3
Apennines, mts. 9 D2, 61 D4, 79 C2
Appleby 67 C3
Ardfert 67 A2
Arezzo 61 C4
Argos 83 B1
Arlaniza 73 C4
Arles 79 A2
Armagh 67 B3
Armenis 83 B3
Arno, r. 61 C4, 79 C2
Arques 55 C4
Arras 55 C5
Arundel 67 C1
Ascoli 61 D4
Assaroe 67 A3
Asti 61 B5
Astorga 72 B4
Athens 9 E1, 83 B1
Athlone 67 B2
Auch 55 C1
Augsburg 79 C4

Aurillac 55 C2
Autun 55 D3
Auxerre 78 A4
Aviero 72 B3
Avila 73 C3
Axios, r. 9 C2
Ayr 67 B3

Badajoz 72 B2
Baeza 73 C2
Balearic Islands 8 C1, 73 E2
Balkan Mts 9 E2, 83 B2
Banff 67 C4
Baños de la Encina 73 C2
Bar 79 A2
Bar 83 B4
Barcelona 73 E3
Barcelona 73 E3
Basle 79 B4
Bayonne 55 B1
Bazas 55 B2
Beaulieu 55 C3
Beaumaris 67 B2
Beaune 79 A3
Beauvais 55 C4
Bedford 67 C2
Beirut 9 F1
Beja 72 B2
Belém 72 A2
Belgrade 9 E2, 83 B2
Belluno 61 D3
Benevento 61 D3
Bere 67 B2
Bergen 89 A3
Berlin 9 D3
Berne 8 C2, 79 B3
Berwick 67 C3
Besalú 73 E4
Besançon 79 B3
Birka 89 B2
Bjelgorod 85 C2
Blagoveschenskii 85 C3
Blanc, Mont 8 C2, 61 B5, 79 B3
Bologna 61 C5
Bonn 8 C3
Bordeaux 55 B2
Bornholm, i. 9 D3
Borovich 85 C3
Boulogne 78 A5
Bourges 55 C3
Boyle 67 A2
Braganca 72 B3
Brandenburg 79 C5
Braslav 85 B3
Bratislava 83 A3
Bremen 79 B6
Brescia 61 C5
Breslau 79 D5, 83 A4
Brest 85 B2
Bridgnorth 67 C2
Brindisi 61 E3
Brive-la-Gaillarde 55 C2
Brixen 79 C3
Bruges 55 C5
Brünn 79 D4
Brussels 8 C3, 79 A5
Bucharest 9 E2, 83 B2
Buchau 79 B4
Budapest 9 D2
Budweis 79 C4, 83 A3
Bug, r. 85 B1
Burgas 83 B2
Burgos 73 C4
Bursa 83 B2
Bury St. Edmunds 67 D2

Cadiz 72 B1
Caen 55 B4
Caernarvon 67 B2
Cagliari 61 C2
Cahors 55 C2

Calahorra 73 D4
Cambrai 79 A5
Cambrian Mts 67 C2
Cambridge 67 C2
Candia 83 B1
Cantabrian Mts 8 B2, 73 C4
Canterbury 67 D1
Capo d'Istria 61 D5
Carcassonne 55 C1
Carlisle 67 C3
Carpathian Mts 9 E2, 83 B3
Carrickfergus 67 B3
Cartagena 73 D1
Caspe 73 D3
Castel del Monte 61 E3
Castelo Branco 72 B2
Castilion 55 B2
Castledermot 67 B2
Catania 61 E1
Cattaro 61 F4
Celanova 72 B4
Cerigo, i. 83 B1
Châlons 55 D4
Channel Islands 8 B2
Charlieu 55 D3
Charroux 55 C3
Chartres 55 C4
Château Gaillard 55 C4
Chernigov 85 C2
Chester 67 C2
Chieti 61 D4
Chinchilla 73 D2
Chinon 55 C3
Chioggia 61 D5
Chios, i. 83 B1
Chur 79 B3
Citeaux 55 D3
Ciudad Real 73 C2
Ciudad Rodrigo 72 B3
Ciudadela 73 E2
Clairvaux 55 D4
Clermont-Ferrand 55 C2
Clitheroe 67 C2
Clonmel 67 B2
Cluj 83 B3
Cluny 55 D3
Coca 73 C3
Coimbra 72 B3
Colchester 67 D1
Cologne 79 B5
Como 61 C5, 79 B3
Compludo 72 B4
Constance 79 B4
Constantinople 83 B2
Conway 67 C2
Copenhagen 9 C3, 89 B2
Corbie 55 C4
Córdoba 73 C1
Corfe 67 C1
Corfu 83 A1
Corfu, i. 83 A1
Coria 72 B2
Cork 67 A1
Corsica, i. 9 C2, 61 C4
Corunna 72 B4
Cosenza 61 E2
Coutances 55 B4
Covadonga 73 C4
Crema 61 C5
Crete, i. 9 E1, 83 B1
Csanad 83 B3
Cuenca 73 D3

Dankov 85 C2
Danube, r. 9 E2, 79 D4, 83 B3
Dax 55 B1
Demirkazik, mt. 9 F1
Deventer 79 B5
Devizes 67 C1
Dijon 55 D3

Dinaric Alps, mts. 9 D2, 83 A2
Disentis 79 B3
Djakovo 83 A3
Dnieper, r. 9 F2, 85 C1
Dniester, r. 9 E2, 83 B3, 85 B1
Dolomites, mts. 9 D2, 79 C3
Don, r. 9 G2
Dordogne, r. 55 C2
Dortmund 79 B5
Dover 67 D1
Drava, r. 9 D2, 79 C3, 83 A3
Drina, r. 9 02
Dubica 83 A3
Dublin 8 B3, 67 B2
Dubrovnik 83 A2
Dumio 72 B3
Dunaverty 67 C3
Dundalk 67 B2
Dunkeath 67 B4
Dunvegan 67 B4
Durazzo 83 A2
Durham 67 C3
Dvina, r. 9 E3, 85 C3
Dynevor 67 C1

Ebro, r. 8 B2, 73 C4
Edinburgh 67 C3
Eger 83 A4
Eger 83 B3
Eileen Donan 67 B4
Elbe, r. 9 D3, 79 C6, 83 A4
Erfurt 79 C5
Essen 79 B5
Esztergom 83 A3
Etampes 55 C4
Etna, Mount 9 D1, 61 D1
Euboea, i. 83 B1
Evora 72 B2
Exeter 67 C1

Fécamp 55 C4
Ferapontov 85 C4
Ferrara 61 C5
Fitero 73 D4
Flavigny 55 D3
Flensburg 89 A1
Fleury 55 C3
Florence 61 C4, 79 C2
Focsani 83 B3
Fontevrault 55 B3
Forfar 67 C4
Fossanova 61 D3
Frangocastello 83 B1
Frankfurt 79 B5
Frankfurt 79 C5
Fulda 79 B5

Galich 85 D3
Gallipoli 83 B2
Galway 67 A2
Garonne, r. 8 B2, 55 C2
Geneva 60 B6, 79 B3
Genoa 61 B5, 79 B2
Gerona 73 E3
Ghent 55 C5
Gibraltar 73 C1
Glastonbury 67 C1
Glogow 83 A4
Gloucester 67 C1
Gmünd 79 B4
Gorizia 79 C3
Gorodets 85 D3
Goslar 79 C5
Gotland, i. 9 D3, 89 B2
Granada 73 C1
Greifswald 79 C6
Grodno 85 B2
Groningen 79 B6
Guadalquivir, r. 8 B1, 73 C1
Guadalupe 73 C2

Guarda 72 B3
Gurk 79 C3
Gyulafehervar 83 B3
Gzhatsk 85 C3

Halicz 85 B1
Halsingborg 89 B2
Hamar 89 B3
Hamburg 79 C6
Hanover 79 B5
Hastings 67 D1
Havelberg 79 C6
Heidelburg 79 B4
Helsinki 9 E4, 89 C3
Hereford 67 C2
Herford 79 B5
Hermitage 67 C3
Holywood 67 B3
Huelgas 73 C4
Huelva 72 B1
Huesca 73 D4
Hylestad 89 A2
Hythe 67 D1

Iasi 83 B3
Idra 83 B1
Iglau 83 A3
Inch 67 B3
Ingolstadt 79 C4
Innsbruck 79 C3
Inverey 67 C4
Inverness 67 B4
Iona 67 B4
Ionian Islands 83 B1

Jaén 73 C1
Ják 83 A3
Jura Mts 8 C2, 79 B3

Kalmar 89 B2
Kalocsa 83 A3
Kaluga 85 C2
Kargopol 85 C4
Karies 83 B2
Karistos 83 B1
Kholm 85 C3
Kiel 79 C6, 89 B1
Kiev 85 C2
Kilia 83 B3
Kilkenny 67 B2
Killala 67 A3
Kirov 85 C2
Kirov 85 D3
Kizil Irmak, r. 9 F1
Klatovy 83 A3
Koblenz 79 B5
Königingrätz 79 D5, 83 A4
Kos, i. 83 B1
Krakow 84 A2
Krasnokholmskii 85 C3
Kungaly 89 B2

La Ferte 55 D3
La Couvertoirade 55 C1
La Rochelle 55 B3
Lamego 72 B3
Lancaster 67 C2
Langres 55 D3
Larisa 83 B2
Lausanne 79 B3
Le Mans 55 C3
Le Puy 55 C2
Leipzig 79 C5
Lelesz 83 B3
Lemnos, i. 83 B1
León 73 C4
Lérida 73 E3
Lesbos, i. 83 B1
Lescar 55 B1
Les Clairets 55 C4

93

Lesina 61 E3
Leyre 73 D4
Limerick 67 A2
Limoges 55 C2
Lincoln 67 C2
Lindau 79 B4
Linkoping 89 B2
Lisbon B1 8, 72 A2
Llandaff 67 C1
Loches 55 C3
Lodève 55 C1
Lodz 84 A2
Loire, r. 8 B2, 55 B3, 79 A3
London 8 C3, 67 D1
Londonderry 67 B3
Lot, r. 55 C2
Lourdes 55 B1
Louvain 79 A5
Luban 79 D5, 83 A4
Lübeck 79 C6
Lublin 85 B2
Lucca 61 C4
Lucera 61 E3
Luckau 83 A4
Lutsk 85 B2
Luxembourg 8 C2, 79 B4
Luxeuil 79 B4
Lvov 85 B1

Mâcon 79 A3
Madrid 8 B2, 73 C3
Majorca, i. 8 C1, 73 E2
Malaga 73 C1
Malmö 89 B2
Mantua 61 C5
Marburg 79 B5
Marienwalde 84 A2
Massif Central, mts. 8 C2, 55 C2
Medina del Campo 73 C3
Meissen 79 C5
Melnik 83 B2
Mende 55 C2
Menderes, r. 9 E1
Mérida 72 B2
Messina 61 E2
Meteora 83 B1
Metz 79 B4
Meuse, r. 8 C2, 79 B5
Milan 61 C5, 79 B3
Minorca, i. 73 E2
Minsk 85 B2
Miranda 72 B3
Mistra 83 B1
Modena 61 C5, 79 C2
Modon 83 B1
Mogilev 85 C2
Moissac 55 C2
Monaco 60 B4, 79 B2
Mondoñedo 72 B4
Monforte 72 B4
Montaner 55 C1
Montereau 55 C3
Monifort 55 C4
Montpellier 55 C1
Mt St. Michel 55 B4
Montserrat 73 E3
Moscow 9 F3, 85 C3
Moulouya, r. 8 B1
Mulhacen, mt. 8 B1
Munich 79 C4
Münster 79 B4
Münster 79 B5
Murcia 73 D1
Murom 85 D3
Musala, mt. 9 E2, 83 B2

Nairn 67 C5
Nantes 55 B3
Naples 61 D3
Narbonne 55 C1

Naxos, i. 83 B1
Neman, r. 9 E3, 85 B3
Nevers 55 C3, 78 A3
Newcastle 67 C3
Newcastle-under-Lyme 67 C2
Nicomedia 83 C2
Nicopolis 83 B2
Nicosia 9 F1
Nikolsevskii Tikhonov 85 D3
Nîmes 55 D1
Nis 83 B2
Nitra 83 A3
Nizhnii Novgorod 85 D3
Nördlingen 79 C4
North Berwick 67 C4
Norwich 67 D2
Nottingham 67 C2
Novgorod 85 C3
Novi Pazar 83 B2
Novogrudok 85 B2

Ochrida 83 B2
Oder, r. 9 D3, 79 C6, 83 A4
Odoyev 85 C2
Ofen 83 A3
Oka, r. 9 G3
Oldenburg 79 B6
Olomouc 79 D4, 83 A3
Olympos, Mt 9 E2, 83 B2
Oporto 72 B3
Oradea 83 B3
Oreshek 85 C3
Orkney Islands 8 B3, 67 C5
Orléans 55 C3
Oslo 9 D3, 89 B2
Osma 73 C3
Osnabruck 79 B5
Otranto 61 F3
Oviedo 73 C4
Oxford 67 C1

Paderborn 79 B5
Paisley 67 B3
Palencia 73 C4
Palermo 61 D2
Palma 73 E2
Pamplona 73 D4
Paris 8 C2, 55 C4
Parma 61 C5
Passau 79 C4
Patras 83 B1
Pec 83 B2
Pécs 83 A3
Pembroke 67 B1
Peñafiel 73 C3
Périgueux 55 C2
Perth 67 C4
Perugia 61 D4
Peterborough 67 C2
Phocaea 83 B1
Piacenca 61 C5, 79 B3
Piedra 73 D3
Pierrefonds 55 C4
Pindus Mts 9 E1, 83 B1
Piombino 61 C4
Pisa 61 C4, 79 C2
Plasencia 72 B3
Plock 84 A2
Plovdiv 83 B2
Po, r. 9 D2, 61 C5, 79 B2
Poblet 73 E3
Poitiers 55 C3
Pola 61 D5
Policastro 61 E3
Polotsk 85 B3
Poltava 85 C1
Pontecorvo 61 D3
Pontigny 55 C3
Pontine Mts 9 F2
Porchester 67 C1

Portalegre 72 B2
Porto Torres 61 B3
Poznan 84 A2
Prague 9 D3, 79 C2, 83 A4
Premontré 55 C4
Pripet, r. 9 E3, 85 B2
Prut, r. 9 E2
Pyrennees, mts. 8 B2, 55 B1, 73 D4

Quedlinburg 79 C5
Quimper 55 A4

Rabat 8 B1
Raciborz 83 A4
Radomsko 84 A2
Ravenna 61 D5
Regensburg 79 C4
Reggio 61 E2
Reims 55 D4
Rennes 55 B4
Rethel 55 D4, 79 A4
Rhine, r. 9 C2, 79 B5
Rhodes 83 B1
Rhodes, i. 9 E1, 83 B1
Rhodope Mts 83 B2
Rhône, r. 8 C2, 61 A5, 79 B3
Ribas de Sil 72 B4
Ribe 89 A2
Richmond 67 C3
Rimini 61 D5
Ripoll 73 E4
Ritzebüttel 79 B6
Rochester 67 D1
Rodez 55 C2
Rome 9 D2, 61 D3
Romney 67 D1
Roscommon 67 A2
Roskilde 89 B2
Rossano 61 E2
Rostock 79 C6
Rostov 85 C3
Rothenburg 79 C4
Rouen 55 C4
Roxburgh 67 C3
Royaumont 55 C4
Rutherglen 67 C3
Ryazan 85 C2

Sahagún 73 C4
Saharan Atlas, mts. 8 C1
St. Albans 67 C1
St Betrand 55 C1
St. Brieuc 55 B4
St. Clair 55 C4
St. David's 67 B1
Saintes 55 B2
St. Evroult 55 C4
St. Maixent 55 B3
St. Omer 55 C5
St. Pol de Léon 55 B4
Salamanca 73 C3
Salerno 61 D3
Salisbury 67 C1
Saluzzo 61 B5
Salzburg 79 C4
Samos 72 B4
San Gimignano 61 C4
S Geronimo de Yuste 73 C3
San Juan de la Peña 73 D4
San Marino 9 D2
San Martin 73 E2
San Sebastian 73 D4
Sandwich 67 D1
Santa Creus 73 E3
Santafé 73 C1
Santander 73 C4
Santiago de Compostela 72 B4
Sao Vincente 72 B1
Saragossa 73 D3

Sarajevo 83 A2
Sardinia, i. 9 D2, 61 C3
Saros 83 B3
Sava, r. 79 D3, 83 A3
Scarborough 67 C3
Schleswig 89 A1
Schweinfurt 79 C5
Sées 55 C4
Segorbe 73 D2
Segovia 73 C3
Seine, r. 8 C2, 55 D4
Senj 83 A3
Sens 55 C4
Seville 72 B1
Shcheremenskii 85 B3
Shetland Islands 8 B4
Shrewsbury 67 C2
Sibenik 83 A2
Siena 61 C4, 79 C2
Sierra Nevada, mts. 8 B1, 73 C1
Sierre 79 B3
Silistria 83 B2
Silves 72 B1
Siret 83 B3
Skara 89 B2
Skog 89 B3
Skopje 83 B2
Smolensk 85 C2
Sofia 9 E2, 83 B2
Segne 89 A3
Soria 73 D3
Speyer 79 B4
Split 61 E4, 83 A2
Squillace 61 E2
Srebrenica 83 A2
Stablo 79 B5
Staroladozhskii 85 C4
Stary Sacz 84 B1
Stavanger 89 A2
Stettin 79 C6
Stirling 67 B4
Stockholm 9 D3, 89 B2
Strasbourg 79 B4
Ströms Vattudal 89 B3
Subiaco 61 D3
Sudenten Mts 74 D5, 83 A4
Suzdal 85 D3
Svendborg 89 B2
Syracuse 61 E1
Szatmar 83 B3

Tagus, r. 8 B1, 72 B2
Taranto 61 E3
Tarazona 73 D3
Tarbert 67 B3
Tarragona 73 E3
Tattershall 67 C2
Taurus Mts 9 F1
Thames, r. 67 C1
Thasos, i. 83 B2
Thessalonica 83 B2
Thouars 55 B3
Tiber, r. 9 D2, 61 D4
Tiranë 9 D2
Tisza, r. 9 E2
Toledo 73 C2
Tonsberg 89 B2
Toplerschlösschen im Rosenthal 79 C4
Tortosa 73 E3
Torzhok 85 C3
Toulouse 55 C1
Tournai 55 C5
Tours 55 C3
Transylvanian Alps, mts. 9 E2, 83 B3
Trelleborg 89 B1
Trent 79 C3
Treviso 61 D5

Trier 79 B4
Trifels 79 B4
Trim 67 B2
Trondheim 89 B3
Troyes 55 D4
Truro 67 B1
Tübingen 79 B4
Tumu Severin 83 B2
Tunis 9 D1
Turin 61 B5, 79 B3
Turku 89 C3
Turov 85 B2
Túy 72 B4
Tver 85 C3

Uppsala 89 B2
Utrecht 79 B5
Uzès 55 D2

Valencia 73 D2
Valladolid 73 C3
Vannes 55 B3
Varberg 89 B2
Varna 83 B2
Vasteras 89 B2
Vaxjo 89 B2
Velikii Ustyug 85 D4
Venice 61 D5
Ventadour 55 C2
Vercelli 61 B5
Vesuvius, Mount 61 D3
Vézelay 55 C3
Viborg 89 A2
Vicenza 61 C5, 79 C3
Vidin 83 B2
Vienna 9 D2, 79 D4
Villandraut 55 B2
Vilna 85 B2
Viseu 72 B3
Vistula, r. 9 D3, 84 B2
Viterbo 61 D4
Vlore 83 A2
Volga, r. 9 F3, 85 D3
Volissos 83 B1
Vologda 85 C3
Vosges Mts 79 B4
Vyborg 89 C3

Waidhofen 79 C4
Waldsassen 79 C5
Warka 85 B2
Warsaw 9 E3, 85 B2
Warwick 67 C2
Waterford 67 B2
Weser, r. 9 C3, 79 C5
Wigtown 67 B3
Winchester 67 C1
Windsor 67 C1
Wisby 89 B2
Wizna 85 B2
Wlodximierz 85 B2
Wschowa 84 A2
Würzburg 79 C4

Yaroslavl 85 C3
Yelets 85 C2
York 67 C2

Zadar 61 E5
Zagreb 83 A3
Zamora 73 C3
Zeitz 79 C5
Zilina 83 A3
Zurich 79 B3

Index

Page numbers in *italics* refer to illustrations or their captions.

Aachen 20
Abbot Suger 44
Africa, North *12*, 16, 17, 26, 72
Agilulf 17
Alaric 15
Alfred *25*
Alps 20
Angevin *see* Plantagenet
Angles 14, 15, *15*
animals 70, *70*
archeological discoveries 22, 90
architecture 42–43, 63, 76, *82*
armies 16, 28, 30, 31, 68, 82
armor *17*, *22*, *31*
arts and crafts 10, 14, *18*, *20*, 24, *38*, 46–47, *46*, *47*, 54, 63
assassination *54*
astrolabes *48*, 53
Athaulph 14
Attila the Hun 15
Augustus (Roman Emperor) 18
Augustus *see* Otto I
Austrasia 20

Baghdad, Siege of *82*
Baltic Sea 24
banking 65
barbarians *12*, 14–15, 16, 17, 26
Basil I and II 26
battles 15, 16–17, *16*, *17*, 63;
    Hastings 28, 31, *33*
Bayeux Tapestry 30–31, *30*, *31*, *52*
Belisarius 16
Benedictine Rule 38
bibles *38*
birds *46*, *47*, *50*, 70;
    see also falconry
Black Sea *87*
bleeding 48
Bohemia 37, 82
books *46*, 50, *52*, *52*, 56, *70*;
    covers *10*, 15, *20*, *47*;
    production 49, 54;
    see also historians; histories; literature
boundaries
    modern political *8–9*;
    territorial 350–1500 C.E. *12*, *13*, *15*, *16*, *17*, *26*, *55*, *61*, *67*, *72*, *73*, *83*, *85*, *89*
Bretwalda see Raedwald

bridges *52*, 58, *62*
British Museum 14, 22
bronze *20*, 22
building methods 38, 42–43, *66*, 68, 86, 90
Bulgars 17, 26, *26*
Burgundians 15, 20, 37, 54, 78, *78*
Burgundy 20, 37
burial customs 22–23, *24*
buried treasure *14*, 22–23
Byzantine Empire *13*, 17, 26–27, *26*, 48
Byzantium *see* Constantinople

campaigns
    of Charlemagne 20;
    of Henry I 37;
    of Justinian 16, 17;
    of Plantagenets 29;
    see also battles; Crusades
capital cities 8, 9, *26*, 72;
    see also settlements
Carolingian Empire 20–21
cartography 74–75
castles 28, *28*, 29, *29*, *31*, *34*, *35*, 37, 66, *67*, 68–69, *78*, 79, 80, *82*, *83*, *85*, *89*
cathedrals 42–45;
    Chartres *43*, 44, *44*, *45*;
    Krakow *84*;
    Lincoln *66*;
    Notre Dame, Paris *44*, 58, *58*, *59*;
    Santa Maria del Fiore, Florence *63*;
    Strasbourg *44*
Catholic church 66, 84
chain mail *31*
Charlemagne (Charles the Great) *12*, 20–21, *20*, 28
Chartres Cathedral *see* cathedrals
Chaucer, Geoffrey 52
children 35, 40, 65
China *52*, 53, *87*
Christianity *12*, *13*, 22, 26, 34–35, 38–39, 44–45, 72, 76, 84, *84*, 88, 90;
    in England *10*;
    in France 15;
    in Ireland *66*;
    in Italy 18;
    in Rome 26;
    in Spain 72
churches 15, 18, *20*, 31, 38, *38*, *39*, 63, 76, 80, *82*, 90, *90*;
    Conques *76*;
    Sacra Croce, Florence *18*;
    Sta. Sophia, Istanbul *27*;
    San Vitale, Ravenna 16, *18*, *18*;

churches (cont'd.)
    Santillana, Spain *76*;
    see also cathedrals; stave churches
Cinque ports 66, *67*
city walls 58, 60, 62, *63*, 72;
    see also fortified cities
clocks 80
cloth 62, *64*, 65, *81*
Clovis 20, 58
Cluny 38
compasses 53
Compostela 56, 76–77
condottieri 60
Conrad of Franconia 36
Constantine the Great 26
Constantinople *12*, *13*, 17, 18, *22*, 24, 26, *27*, 63, 82
cooking 81
cotton *64*
crossbows *35*
crosses *20*, 38, *66*, 86
crowns 15
Crusades *13*, 34–35, *34*, 54, 63, 64, *82*
Czechs 82

Danelaw *25*
Danes 28, 68
Dante Alighieri 63
Denmark 88
Diocletian *12*, *13*
Domesday Book 32–33
dyes 63

East Anglia 24
East Roman Empire *see* Byzantine Empire; Roman Empire
education 40–41;
    see also universities
Edward the Confessor 28, 30, *30*, *33*, 66
Emperors *see* Roman Emperors
empires *see* Carolingian; Frankish; Holy Roman Empire; Justinian; Plantagenet; Roman
enamel *20*
entertainment *47*, *49*, 52
European Union (EU) 8
everyday life 70, *70*, 80, 86–87

fairs *64*, 65
falconry *50*, *70*
farm buildings *25*
farming 33, *33*, *54*, 62, 70, *70*
Flanders 78
Florence 62–63
food *64*, *65*, *70*, *81*, 88
fortified cities and towns 16, *17*, 35, 36, 37, 56, *56*, *57*, 62, *62*, 68, *73*, 90

Frankish Empire *12*, *13*
Franks *12*, *13*, 15, *15*, 20, *52*
Frederick of Germany 35
furs 24, 88
fustian *64*

Gaul 14, 20
Genghis Khan *87*
Genoa 63, *65*
Geoffrey of Anjou 28
German Empire *see* Holy Roman Empire
glass 44;
    stained 44–45
gold (metal) 26, *64*, 82
gold (objects) *14*, *20*
Gothic style 42–43
Goths 14, 15, *18*
government 81;
    in England 66;
    in France 54–55, 68;
    in Germany 78;
    in Italy 60–61, 62, 63;
    in the Low Countries 78;
    in Switzerland 78;
    in Wales 66
grain *64*, 65
Greece 82
Greek classics 63
Greeks *18*, 74
guilds 62, 65, 81
Gutenberg, Johann 49

Hanse (Hanseatic League) 88
Hapsburgs 78
Harald of Norway 30
Harold (Norman King) 28, 30, *30*, 31, *31*
heathens 24
helmets 20, 31
Henry I of Saxony 36, 37
Henry II of England 28, *28*, 29
Henry the Navigator 75
historians
    Ammianus Marcellinus 14;
    Bishop of Freising *57*;
    Froissart 58;
    Ordericus of Vitalis 40;
    Procopius 14
histories 32;
    Anglo-Saxon Chronicle 24, *32*;
    Book of Marvels 52;
    see also Bayeux Tapestry; Domesday Book
Holy Land *13*, 34, 72
Holy Roman Empire *13*, 36–37, *37*, 78, *78*, 82
honey 24
houses 25, *66*, 91
Hungary 82
Huns 15, *15*, 17
hunting 28, 56, 70, *70*

icons *84*
illness 48, *49*
illuminated manuscripts *10*
India *87*
industries 80, *81*;
    see also cloth; pottery; wool
Ireland 66
Islam *12*, *13*, 26, 72
ivory *10*, *47*

jewelry 15, *18*
Justinian 14, 16–17, *16*, *17*, *18*, 26, *26*
Jutes 14, 15, *15*

Khusrau I 17
kings
    Anglo-Saxon *25*;
    Bohemian 82;
    Carolingian 20;
    Danish 88;
    East Anglian 22;
    English 28, 29, 30, 35, 88;
    Frankish 20, 58;
    French 35, 54–55;
    German 16, 35, 36–37;
    Lombard 17;
    Norwegian 30;
    Ostrogoth 15, 16, 18;
    Polish *84*;
    Spanish 35, 60
knights *34*, 35;
    St. John the Hospitalers 35, 56, 82;
    Templars 35, 56;
    Teutonic 35, 37

Lanfranc 40
languages 20, 36, 49
law (teaching of) 40, 63
leather *22*, 64
leeches 48
Leonardo da Vinci 48, *48*
Lindau Gospels *20*
Lindisfarne *10*, 24
Lindisfarne Gospels *10*
linen 30, 64
literature 46–47, 50, *52*, 63;
    classics 20
Lithuania 84
Lombards 17, *17*, 37, 60
longships 24, 31, *52*
Louis IX 35, *44*, 54
Luxembourgs 78
lyre *22*

Macedonians 26
Magyars 36, 37
Manuel I 26
manuscripts 20, 37, 40, *41*, *47*, 54
maps 53, 74–75
markets *see* fairs
Martel, Charles 20

mathematics 74
Matilda 28
Maximian *12*
Medici family 60, 63
medicine 40, 48, *49*, 63
Mediterranean Sea 64
mercenaries 14, 60
metalwork *14*, 15, 37, 64
Middle East 26
Mieszko I 84
monasteries 20, 38, *41*, 52, *54*, *55*, *67*, *72*, *73*, *77*, *78*, *79*, *83*, *85*, *89*
monastic life 38, 47
money changing *65*
Mongols *82*, 84, *87*
monks 38, *40*, 42, 44
mosaics *16*, *18*
mosques 27
mother-of-pearl *18*
motte-and-bailey *see* castles
mountain ranges 8, *8*, *9*
music 40, 47, *47*, 52
Muslims 12, *13*, 17, 20, 26, 34, *35*, 48, 54, 72, 76, 82

Narbonne 15
Narses 16
nation states *13*
navigation 48, 74
Neustria 20
Normans 28, 30–31, 42–43, *66*, 66, 69
North America 24, *24*, *25*
nuns 38

Odo of Bayeux *30*, *31*, 33
Ordovacar 16
Ostrogoths 14, 15, *15*, 17, 18, 20
Otto I 36, 37

Ottoman Turks *13*, 17, 26, 82

pack animals 65
pagan burial 22
paganism 88
Paris 58–59
parliament 54, 66
pattern books 46
peoples *13*, *15*, *16*, *17*, 37
Pepin III 20
perfumes 63
Persians 17
Philip II of France 35
philosophy 40
pilgrimages 34–35, 52, *56*, 64, 76–77, *77*
piracy 64
place names 66
plainchant (plainsong) 47
Plantagenet Empire 28, 29
playing cards *49*
plowing *33*, *70*
Poland 84
Pomerania, Duchy of 37
Pompeii *18*
popes 20, 38;
    Gregory I (the Great) *10*, *47*;
    Gregory VI 36;
    Gregory VII *37*;
    Leo III *20*, 26;
    Urban II 34
populations *66*, 80;
    Roman Empire 12
Portugal 26, 72, *74*, *75*
pottery 80
precious stones 63
printing 49, *49*, 74
Procopius 14
Prussia 37

Raedwald 22

Ravenna 15, 16, 18–19
religion *see* Christianity; Islam
religious objects 34
Richard I 35
roads 52, 66
Roman army 16
Roman Britain 14
Roman emperors *12*, *13*, 15, 16–17, 18
Roman Empire *12*, *13*, 15, 16–17, 26, 38, 48, 60;
    see also Byzantine Empire
Roman navy 18
Romanesque style *76*
Romans 8, 12, 14, 15, 72
Rome 16, 34, *60*
rose window 43, *44*
Russia 84, 87

saints 76
Saladin 35
Saracen Turks 20
Saxons 14, 15, *15*, 20, 28, *33*, *66*, 68
Scandinavia 88
science *47*, 48
sculpture 46
sea charts 74
seafaring 24
Seljuks 26
settlements, major 350–1500 C.E. *12*, *13*, *16*, *17*, *24*, *25*, *29*, *35*, *61*, *67*, *72*, *73*, *78*, *79*, *83*, *85*, *89*
sheep 25
shields 22
shipbuilding *24*, *31*
ships *22*, *23*, *24*, *31*, *52*, 65
sieges 16, *35*, *87*
Silesia, Duchy of 37
silk *64*

silver (metal) 24, 82
silver (objects) *14*, *22*
slaves 23, 33, 35
Slavs 13, 17, 36, 37
Spain 26, *64*, 72–73, *76*
spears *22*, 35
spices *62*, 63, *64*
spinning wheels 80
stained glass 44–45, *81*
statues *20*, *27*
stave churches 90, *90*
Stephen 28, 29, *29*
stonemasons 42, *42*, 46, 63
Strasbourg Cathedral *see* cathedrals
Suevi *15*
sugar 64
Sutton Hoo 22–23
Sweden 88
Switzerland 78
swords *22*
Syria 26

taxes 52, 66, 90
teaching 40–41;
    see also law; universities
technology 48–49;
    see also building methods
Templar Knights 35, *56*
tesserae 18
Teutonic Knights 35, 37
textiles 64–65, *64*
Theodora 18, *18*
Theodoric 15, 16, *16*, 18
Theodosius *12*, 15, 26, 38
Thetford treasure *14*
timber 24, *64*, 65, 86
towns *see* fortified cities and towns; houses; villages
trade 16, 24, *58*, 62, 63, 64–65, *81*, 88
trades 37, 65;
    see also cloth; industries

transport 52–53, 65, 86
travel 52–53;
    see also ships; trade
Trelleborg *91*
troubadours 47

universities 40, 54, *54*, *55*, *78*, *79*, *83*, *84*, *85*, *89*

Vandals 15, *15*, 16, 26
Vatican 20
Venetian ports 65, *68*
Venice 60, 63
Vikings 24–25
villages 86–87;
    see also everyday life
Viscontis 60
Visigoths 14, 15, *15*, 20
volcanic eruption *25*

Wales 66, 68
warships 24, 31, *33*
water mills 80
weapons *22*, 31, *31*, 35
West Roman Empire *see* Roman Empire
William the Conqueror 30–33, *31*, 52
windmills 80
wine *64*, 88
women 65, *81*
wood carvers 46, *80*, 86, 90
wool industry 64, *64*, 88
Worms 15

York *66*